2011

中国国际收支报告
China's Balance of Payments Report

国家外汇管理局国际收支分析小组
BOP Analysis Group
State Administration of Foreign Exchange

中国金融出版社
China Financial Publishing House

责任编辑：张翠华
责任校对：孙　蕊
责任印制：裴　刚

图书在版编目（CIP）数据

2011 中国国际收支报告（2011 Zhongguo Guoji Shouzhi Baogao）／国家外汇管理局国际收支分析小组 . —北京：中国金融出版社，2012.9
ISBN 978-7-5049-6515-8

Ⅰ . ① 2··· 　Ⅱ . ①国··· 　Ⅲ . ①国际收支—研究报告—中国—2011
Ⅳ . ① F812.4

中国版本图书馆 CIP 数据核字（2012）第 170200 号

出版
发行　　中国金融出版社

社址　　北京市丰台区益泽路 2 号
市场开发部　　（010）63266347，63805472，63439533　（传真）
网上书店　http://www.chinafph.com　　（010）63286832，63365686　（传真）
读者服务部　　（010）66070833，62568380
邮编　　100071
经销　　新华书店
印刷　　北京汇林印务有限公司
尺寸　　210 毫米 ×285 毫米
印张　　11.25
字数　　125 千
版次　　2012 年 9 月第 1 版
印次　　2012 年 9 月第 1 次印刷
印数　　1—2000
定价　　80.00 元
ISBN 978-7-5049-6515-8/F.6075
如出现印装错误本社负责调换　　联系电话：（010）63263947

国家外汇管理局
国际收支分析小组人员名单

组　　长：易　纲

副 组 长：邓先宏　方上浦　王小奕　李　超　杨国中　黄国波　韩玉婷

审　　稿：刘　薇　杜　鹏　孙鲁军　王允贵　王春英　崔汉忠

统　　稿：管　涛　方　文　温建东　周　济

执　　笔：

第一部分：王彩玲　马　昀　赵玉超　高　铮

第二部分：吕　晓　李玲青　吴　昊　韩　健

第三部分：贾　宁　龙　芳

第四部分：王彩玲　马　昀

专　　栏：马　昀　温建东　贾　宁　谢月兰　王彩玲

附录整理：孙刚强

英文翻译：周海文　王　亮　胡　红

英文审校：Nancy Hearst（美国哈佛大学费正清东亚研究中心）

Contributors to This Report

Head
Yi Gang

Deputy Head
Deng Xianhong   Fang Shangpu   Wang Xiaoyi   Li Chao
Yang Guozhong   Huang Guobo   Han Yuting

Readers
Liu Wei   Du Peng   Sun Lujun   Wang Yungui
Wang Chunying   Cui Hanzhong

Editors
Guan Tao   Fang Wen   Wen Jiandong   Zhou Ji

Authors
Part One: Wang Cailing   Ma Yun   Zhao Yuchao   Gaozheng
Part Two: Lv Xiao   Li Lingqing   Wu Hao   Han Jian
Part Three: Jia Ning   Long Fang
Part Four: Wang Cailing   Ma Yun
Boxes: Ma Yun   Wen Jiandong   Jia Ning   Xie Yuelan
          Wang Cailing

Appendix: Sun Gangqiang

Translators: Zhou Haiwen   Wang Liang   Hu Hong

Proofreader: Nancy Hearst (Fairbank Center for East Asian
          Research, Harvard University)

内容摘要

2011 年，国内外环境复杂多变。国际上，欧美债务危机不断发酵，世界经济增长明显放缓，国际金融市场动荡加剧；从国内看，国民经济继续朝着宏观调控的预期方向发展，经济增速温和回落，物价涨幅得到初步控制，经济增长的内生性进一步增强。

2011 年，我国克服国内外不稳定、不确定因素的影响，涉外经济继续保持健康发展势头。对外经济交往更加活跃，全年国际收支交易总规模较 2010 年增长 22%。国际收支继续保持经常项目与资本项目"双顺差"，其中，经常项目顺差 2 017 亿美元，资本和金融项目顺差 2 211 亿美元。国际收支状况进一步改善，经常项目顺差与国内生产总值之比为 2.8%，较 2010 年下降 1.2 个百分点；国际收支总顺差 4 228 亿美元，下降 19%。跨境资本流动波动较大，由前三季度资本净流入同比增长 62%，转为第四季度净流出 290 亿美元；交易形成的外汇储备增加额由前三季度同比多增 888 亿美元，转为全年少增 847 亿美元。

2012 年，预计我国国际收支仍总体保持顺差格局，但顺差规模将继续稳步回落，短期波动可能加大。下一阶段，外汇管理工作将把握好"稳中求进"的工作总基调，巩固和扩大应对国际金融危机冲击成果，进一步提高外汇管理服务实体经济的能力，稳步推进贸易外汇管理等重点领域改革，防范和打击"热钱"流入，促进国民经济平稳较快发展。

Abstract

In 2011 the domestic and external economic environments were both complicated and ever–changing. Internationally, the sovereign debt crisis in Europe and the United States deteriorated, leading to slower economic growth globally and fluctuations in international financial markets. Domestically, the Chinese economy developed as directed by the macro controls, with a slight drop in economic growth, inflation, and intensified endogenous growth.

In 2011 China's external economy maintained its healthy development despite the influence of both domestic and external volatilities and uncertainties. External economic relations became more active, with the total volume of balance of payments transactions increasing by 22 percent year on year. The balance of payments achieved a surplus in both the current account and the capital and financial account. In particular, the current account surplus totaled USD 201.7 billion, and the capital and financial account surplus totaled USD 221.1 billion. The status of the balance of payments further improved: the ratio of the current account surplus to GDP was 2.8 percent, down 1.2 percentage points from that in 2010; the total BOP surplus was USD 422.8 billion, decreasing by 19 percent year on year. Cross–border capital flows fluctuated, growing by 62 percent year on year in the first three quarters but then producing a net outflow of USD 29 billion in the fourth quarter. Although in the first three quarters, growth in foreign reserve transactions was USD 88.8 billion more than that in the first three quarters of 2010, growth in foreign reserves for the entire year was USD 84.7 billion less than that in 2010.

As forecasted, the surplus in the balance of payments in 2012 will remain, with a descending momentum and more rapid fluctuations in the short term. During the next stage, the foreign exchange administration authorities will maintain progress with stability, reinforce and expand measures to protect against the international financial crisis, further improve foreign exchange administration to serve the real economy, promote key reforms including foreign trade administration, fight against hot money inflows, and promote steady and rapid economic development.

目 录

专栏

图

表

Contents

Boxes

Charts

Tables

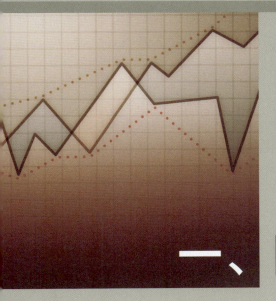

一、国际收支概况

（一）国际收支运行环境

2011 年，全球经济增长明显放缓，国际金融动荡加剧。据国际货币基金组织最新测算，2011 年全球经济增速从 2010 年的 5.2% 下滑至 3.8%，其中主要发达国家经济体增速由 3.2% 下滑至 1.6%，新兴经济体经济增速由 7.3% 回落到 6.2%。全球货币政策回归宽松，并逐渐由防范通胀和资产泡沫风险，转向刺激经济、稳定金融（见表 1-1）。随着欧美债务危机不断发酵，国际金融市场大幅震荡，下半年全球投资风险偏好下降，新兴市场经济体普遍由资本流入、本币升值转为资本流出、本币贬值（见图 1-1，有关讨论详见专栏 4）。

表 1-1　2011 年部分经济体货币政策动态

国家或地区	货币政策动态
欧元区	2011 年 4 月、7 月分别上调基准再融资利率 25 个基点至 1.5%，11 月、12 月各下调 25 个基点至 1%。
澳大利亚	2011 年 11 月、12 月各下调基准利率 25 个基点至 4.25%。
挪威	2011 年 5 月上调基准利率至 2.25%，12 月下调基准利率 0.5 个百分点至 1.75%。这是该国 2009 年 10 月以来首次降息，幅度超预期。
中国	2011 年 1-6 月各上调存款类金融机构人民币存款准备金率 0.5 个百分点至 21%；2 月、4 月、7 月各上调存贷款基准利率 25 个基点。11 月 30 日下调存款类金融机构人民币存款准备金率 0.5 个百分点。
巴西	2011 年 3 月、4 月各上调 SELIC 隔夜利率 50 个基点，7 月上调 25 个基点至 12.5%。8 月、10 月和 11 月分别下调 0.5% 至 11%。
印度尼西亚	2011 年 2 月上调 BI 利率 25 个基点。10 月下调 25 个基点，11 月下调 50 个基点至 6%。
泰国	2011 年 1 月、3 月各上调基准利率 25 个基点。11 月下调 25 个基点至 3.25%。

2011 年以来，我国经济继续朝着宏观调控的预期方向发展。经济增速温和回落，全年国内生产总值（GDP）增长 9.2%，较上年回落 1.2 个百分点；物价涨幅得到初步抑制，居民消费价格（CPI）总水平在 7 月达到年内峰值后逐月回落，全年消费价格涨幅为 5.4%（见图 1-2）。拉动中国经济增长的"三驾马车"动力更为协调，资本形成总额对经济增长的贡献率是 54.2%，最终消费对经济增长的贡献率是 51.6%，内需对我国经济增长的贡献率比 2010 年大幅上升。货币政策方面，前三季度，面对通货膨胀压力不断加大的形势，先后 6 次上调存款准备金率、3 次上调存贷款基准利率（见图 1-3）；9 月以后适时采取了一系列措施进行微调（包括 11 月 30 日下调一次存款准备金率），适当增加市场流动性，保持了货币信贷总体适度。

图 1-1

2010—2011 年新兴市场货币指数、股票价格指数与 Libor—OIS 利差

新兴市场股票价格指数MSCI ── 新兴市场货币指数EMCI ── Libor—OIS利差（右轴）

注：MSCI、EMCI 以 2010 年 1 月 1 日为基期；3 个月美元伦敦同业市场拆借利率（Libor）与隔夜指数掉期（OIS）之间的利差（基点）反映全球银行体系的信贷压力。
数据来源：彭博资讯。

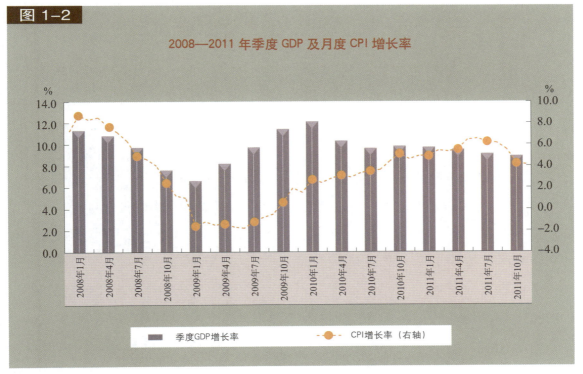

图 1-2

2008—2011 年季度 GDP 及月度 CPI 增长率

季度GDP增长率 ── CPI增长率（右轴）

数据来源：国家统计局。

图 1-3

2008—2011 年金融机构存款准备金率及一年期存款利率

金融机构存款准备金率 —— 金融机构一年期存款利率（右轴）

数据来源：中国人民银行。

专栏 1

2011 年主要涉外经济政策调整

2011 年，我国加快转变经济发展方式，外贸、外资和外汇领域的政策调整取得成效，国际收支状况进一步趋向平衡。主要措施包括：

贸易政策："稳出口、扩进口"，促进贸易平衡和结构升级。取消部分钢材、有色金属加工材等 406 个税号的退税率，抑制"两高一资"及部分农产品出口。积极扩大进口，自 7 月 1 日起先后取消或大幅下调汽油、柴油等原材料，以及千万吨炼油设备、天然气管道运输设备等重大技术设备的进口关税和增值税。在戛纳峰会上宣布，对同中国建立外交关系的最不发达国家的 97% 税目产品给予零关税待遇。公布《关于 2012 年关税实施方案的通知》，明确适用进口暂定税率的 730 多种商品平均税率为 4.4%，比最惠国税率低 50% 以上。加快加工贸易转型升级的步伐，通过税收杠杆鼓励来料加工企业转型为法人企业。发布《服务贸易发展"十二五"规划纲要》，提高服务贸易在对外贸易中的比重。

直接投资和金融政策：规范和引导并重，促进"引进来"与"走出去"双向合理发展。建立我国跨部门的外国投资者并购境内企业安全审查制度，出台相关管理规定。修改《外商直接投资产业指导目录》，鼓励外商投资现代化农业、现代服务业和文化领域。综合运用多种措施支持国内企业开展对外直接投资，进一步下放境外投资项目核准权限。用好非洲中小企业发展专项贷款，支持国内企业对非开展直接投资。允许境内机构以人民币对外投资、境外投资者以人民币到境内开展直接投资，明确商业银行开展境外项目人民币贷款条件，支持企业"走出去"。允许境内金融机构到香港等境外市场发行人民币债券。

外汇管理政策：统筹防风险和便利化，促进经济平稳较快发展。切实把减缓银行结售汇顺差过快增长作为中心工作，启动应对异常跨境资金流入预案，加强银行结售汇头寸、出口收结汇、短期外债等外汇业务管理。发挥外汇检查手段的作用，集中力量查办重大违规案件。2011年，共查处外汇违法违规案件3488件，收缴罚没款达到5亿元人民币，较2010年增长1倍多；破获39起地下钱庄、非法买卖外汇等违法犯罪案件，涉案金额合计达717亿元人民币。同时，稳步推进进出口核销制度改革，降低企业和银行财务成本；将出口收入存放境外政策推广至全国，便利经济主体持有外汇；下放贸易信贷、对外担保等五项业务的审批权限，便利个人通过电子银行渠道办理结售汇业务；发布人民币合格境外投资者境内证券投资业务试点办法，有序拓宽资本市场开放；大力引导外汇市场产品创新和业务发展，推出人民币对外汇期权交易。

（二）国际收支主要状况

国际收支继续保持"双顺差"，顺差规模有所减少。2011年，我国经常项目顺差2 017亿美元，同比下降15%，资本和金融项目顺差2 211亿美元，下降23%[①]；国际收支总顺差4 228亿美元，较2010年下降19%，低于2007—2010年年均顺差4 686亿美元的规模（见表1-2）。

---

① 根据最新获得的外商投资企业联合年检汇总"两未"利润（即未分配利润、已分配未汇出利润）数据，对2010年国际收支平衡表进行了修订。由于2007—2009年外商投资企业利润率较低，导致对2010年"两未"利润的估算偏低，现根据2010年年检实得数据进行了调整。

表1-2　2005—2011年国际收支顺差结构　　　　　　　　　　　　　　　　　　　　　　单位：亿美元

项　目	2005年	2006年	2007年	2008年	2009年	2010年	2011年
国际收支总差额	2 351	2 854	4 491	4 587	4 420	5 247	4 228
经常项目差额	1 341	2 327	3 540	4 124	2 611	2 378	2 017
占国际收支总差额比重（%）	57.0	81.5	78.8	89.9	59.1	45.3	47.7
与GDP之比（%）	5.9	8.6	10.1	9.1	5.2	4.0	2.8
资本和金融项目差额	1 010	526	951	463	1 808	2 869	2 211
占国际收支总差额比重（%）	43.0	18.4	21.2	10.1	40.9	54.7	52.3
与GDP之比（%）	4.5	1.9	2.7	1.0	3.6	4.8	3.0

数据来源：国家外汇管理局，国家统计局。

　　货物贸易顺差略有下降。按国际收支统计口径，2011年，我国货物贸易出口19 038亿美元，进口16 603亿美元，分别较2010年增长20%和25%；货物贸易顺差2 435亿美元，下降4%[①]（见图1-4）。

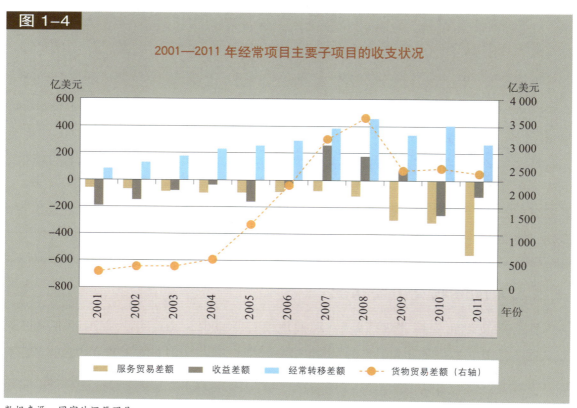

图1-4

2001—2011年经常项目主要子项目的收支状况

服务贸易差额　　收益差额　　经常转移差额　　货物贸易差额（右轴）

数据来源：国家外汇管理局。

---

① 本口径与海关口径的主要差异在于，一是海关统计的到岸价进口额按5%减去其中的运输和保险费用后计为国际收支口径的进口，二是国际收支口径还包括货物修理、运输工具在港口购买的货物以及抓获的进出口走私，并分别在进出口中扣除了退货。

服务贸易逆差迅速扩大。2011 年，我国服务贸易收入 1 828 亿美元，较 2010 年增长 13%；服务贸易支出 2 381 亿美元，增长 23%；逆差 552 亿美元，增长 77%。全年，货物与服务贸易顺差合计为 1 883 亿美元，较上年下降 16 %，与 GDP 之比为 2.6%，延续了 2007 年以来见顶回落的走势（见图 1-5）。

图 1-5

1994—2011 年货物和服务贸易差额与 GDP 之比

数据来源：国家外汇管理局。

收益项目逆差下降。2011 年，收益项目收入 1 446 亿美元，较 2010 年增长 2%；支出 1 565 亿美元，下降 7%；逆差 119 亿美元，下降 54%。其中，投资收益逆差 268 亿美元，下降 30%；职工报酬净流入 150 亿美元，较 2010 年增长 23%。

直接投资顺差下降。2011 年，直接投资顺差 1 704 亿美元，较 2010 年下降 8%。其中，外国来华直接投资净流入 2 201 亿美元，下降 10%；我国对外直接投资净流出 497 亿美元，下降 14%（见图 1-6）。

证券投资净流入较快下降。2011 年，证券投资项下净流入 196 亿美元，较 2010 年下降 18%。其中，我国对外证券投资净回流 62 亿美元，2010 年为净流出 76 亿美元；境外对我国证券投资净流入 134 亿美元，减少 58%。

其他投资净流入大幅下降。2011 年，其他投资项下净流入 255 亿美元，较 2010 年下降 65%。其中，我国企业和银行对外赊账或存放款，导致其他投资项下对外资产净增加 1 668 亿美元，增长 43%；境外对我国企业和银行赊账或存放款，导致其他投资项下对外负债净增加 1 923 亿美元，增长 2%。

图 1-6

2001—2011 年资本和金融项目主要子项目的收支状况

数据来源：国家外汇管理局。

儲备资产增长放缓。2011 年，剔除汇率、价格等非交易价值变动影响（下同），

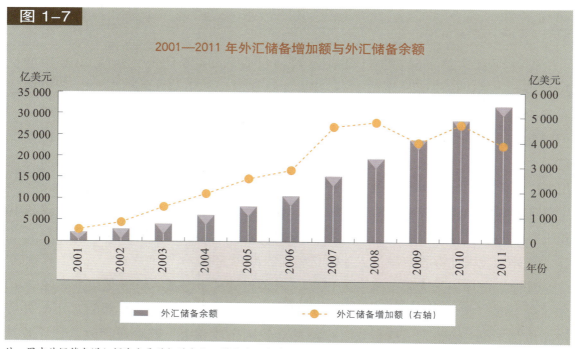

图 1-7

2001—2011 年外汇储备增加额与外汇储备余额

注：图中外汇储备增加额为交易引起的变化，剔除了估值效应的影响。
数据来源：国家外汇管理局。

我国新增储备资产 3 878 亿美元。其中，外汇储备增加 3 848 亿美元，较 2010 年少增 847 亿美元，低于 2007—2010 年年均增加 4 477 亿美元的规模（见图 1-7）；我国在基金组织的储备头寸净增加 34 亿美元。

净误差与遗漏额为负。2011 年，净误差与遗漏为借方 350 亿美元，占国际收支口径货物进出口总额的 –1%，远低于 ±5% 的国际标准（见图 1-8）。误差与遗漏的产生主要是由于数据来源的多样化，各种数据在统计口径、统计时间和计价标准等方面存在不一致。2001 年以来，净误差与遗漏有 5 年出现在借方、6 年在贷方，方向是随机的，与"热钱"流出流入没有必然的联系（具体讨论详见《2005 年上半年中国国际收支报告》专栏 2）。

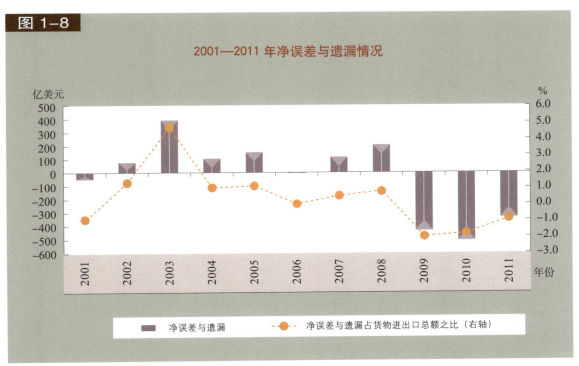

图 1-8

2001—2011 年净误差与遗漏情况

■ 净误差与遗漏 　　●--- 净误差与遗漏占货物进出口总额之比（右轴）

数据来源：国家外汇管理局。

表 1-3　2011 年中国国际收支平衡表[①]　　　　　　　　　　　　　　单位：亿美元

项　目	差　额	贷　方	借　方
一、经常项目	2 017	22 868	20 851
A. 货物和服务	1 883	20 867	18 983
a. 货物	2 435	19 038	16 603
b. 服务	–552	1 828	2 381

———————————
① 我国国际收支平衡表按国际货币基金组织《国际收支手册》第五版规定的各项原则编制，采用复式记账原则记录所有发生在我国居民（不包括港、澳、台地区）与非居民之间的经济交易。本表计数采用四舍五入原则。

续表

项　目	差　额	贷　方	借　方
1. 运输	-449	356	804
2. 旅游	-241	485	726
3. 通讯服务	5	17	12
4. 建筑服务	110	147	37
5. 保险服务	-167	30	197
6. 金融服务	1	8	7
7. 计算机和信息服务	83	122	38
8. 专有权利使用费和特许费	-140	7	147
9. 咨询	98	284	186
10. 广告、宣传	12	40	28
11. 电影、音像	-3	1	4
12. 其他商业服务	140	323	183
13. 别处未提及的政府服务	-3	8	11
B. 收益	**-119**	**1 446**	**1 565**
1. 职工报酬	150	166	16
2. 投资收益	-268	1 280	1 549
C. 经常转移	**253**	**556**	**303**
1. 各级政府	-26	0	26
2. 其他部门	278	556	277
二、资本和金融项目	**2 211**	**13 982**	**11 772**
A. 资本项目	**54**	**56**	**2**
B. 金融项目	**2 156**	**13 926**	**11 770**
**　1. 直接投资**	**1 704**	**2 717**	**1 012**
1.1 我国在外直接投资	-497	174	671
1.2 外国在华直接投资	2 201	2 543	341
**　2. 证券投资**	**196**	**519**	**323**
2.1 资产	62	255	192
2.1.1 股本证券	11	112	101
2.1.2 债务证券	51	143	91
2.1.2.1（中）长期债券	50	137	88
2.1.2.2 货币市场工具	2	5	4
2.2 负债	134	265	131
2.2.1 股本证券	53	152	99
2.2.2 债务证券	81	113	32

续表

项　目	差　额	贷　方	借　方
2.2.2.1（中）长期债券	30	61	32
2.2.2.2 货币市场工具	51	51	0
3. 其他投资	**255**	**10 690**	**10 435**
3.1 资产	−1 668	1 088	2 756
3.1.1 贸易信贷	−710	0	710
长期	−14	0	14
短期	−695	0	695
3.1.2 贷款	−453	61	513
长期	−433	8	441
短期	−20	53	73
3.1.3 货币和存款	−987	501	1 489
3.1.4 其他资产	482	526	44
长期	0	0	0
短期	482	526	44
3.2 负债	1 923	9 602	7 679
3.2.1 贸易信贷	380	454	74
长期	6	8	1
短期	374	447	73
3.2.2 贷款	1 051	7 343	6 292
长期	130	538	408
短期	920	6 805	5 884
3.2.3 货币和存款	483	1 719	1 237
3.2.4 其他负债	10	86	76
长期	−15	24	39
短期	24	61	37
三、储备资产	**−3 878**	**10**	**3 888**
1. 货币黄金	0	0	0
2. 特别提款权	5	5	0
3. 在基金组织的储备头寸	−34	6	40
4. 外汇	−3 848	0	3 848
5. 其他债权	0	0	0
四、净误差与遗漏	**−350**	**0**	**350**

数据来源：国家外汇管理局。

（三）国际收支运行评价

2011 年，我国涉外经济活动继续保持较快增长。全年国际收支交易总规模为 6.95 万亿美元，创历史新高，较上年增长 22%；与同期 GDP 之比为 95%，占比较上年下降 0.6 个百分点（见图 1-9）。

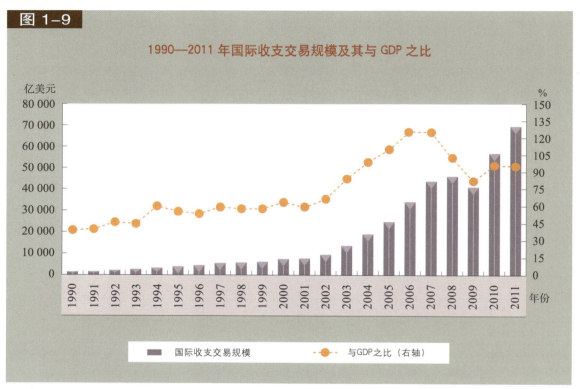

图 1-9

1990—2011 年国际收支交易规模及其与 GDP 之比

数据来源：国家外汇管理局，国家统计局。

跨境资本流动日趋活跃。2011 年，资本和金融项目交易规模 2.58 万亿美元，占我国国际收支总规模的 37%（见图 1-10）；经常项目交易规模 4.37 万亿美元，占我国国际收支交易总规模的 63%，与资本和金融项目交易规模占比相差 26 个百分点，差距较 2001 年缩小了 32 个百分点。2011 年，资本和金融项目顺差占国际收支总顺差的 52%，连续第二年超过经常项目顺差成为外汇储备增加的主要来源（见表 1-2）。

经常项目收支状况进一步改善。2011 年，我国经常项目顺差较上年下降 15%，与 GDP 之比为 2.8%，较 2010 年下降 1.2 个百分点（见图 1-11）。2008 年以来，我国经常项目顺差与 GDP 之比逐步降至国际公认的合理区间（见专栏 2），既体现了国内经济发展方式转变、涉外经济政策调整的成效，也反映了国外经济金融形势的变化，还显示人民币汇率正逐渐趋于合理均衡水平。

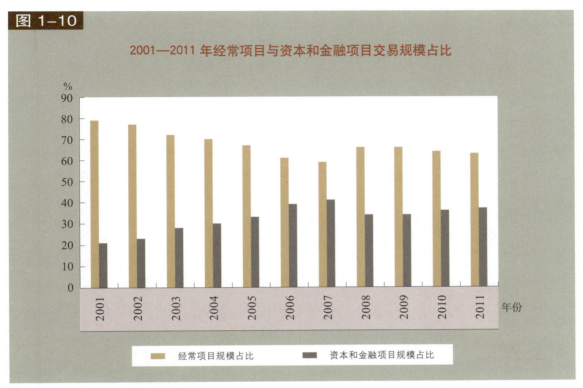

图 1-10

2001—2011 年经常项目与资本和金融项目交易规模占比

经常项目规模占比　　　　资本和金融项目规模占比

数据来源：国家外汇管理局，国家统计局。

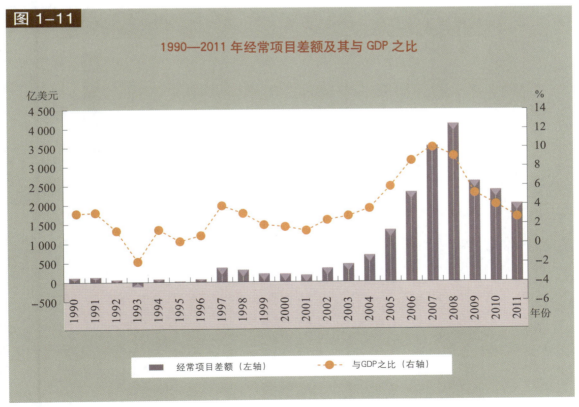

图 1-11

1990—2011 年经常项目差额及其与 GDP 之比

经常项目差额（左轴）　　　与GDP之比（右轴）

数据来源：海关总署，国家统计局。

专栏 2

关于国际收支平衡状况的度量

    国际收支平衡，也称对外经济平衡，是宏观经济四大目标之一。在开放经济条件下，国内均衡和对外均衡之间存在着密切的相互决定、相互影响的关系。如果增长、就业和物价没有达到均衡状态，必然会反映到国际收支上来；如果国际收支很不平衡，就不可能真正充分利用两个市场、两种资源，也就不可能真正扩大就业，促进经济社会协调发展。

    在实践中，国际收支平衡的主要评判标准是经常项目差额是否可持续。在资本账户开放的经济体，资本项目通常是经常项目的对冲项，经常项目逆差时资本净流入，经常项目顺差时则资本净流出（见图 C2-1）。相关国家国际收支危机的教训是，经常项目逆差是否超过 GDP 的 4%～5% 是一个非常关

图 C2-1

2010 年部分国家经常与资本项目差额与 GDP 之比

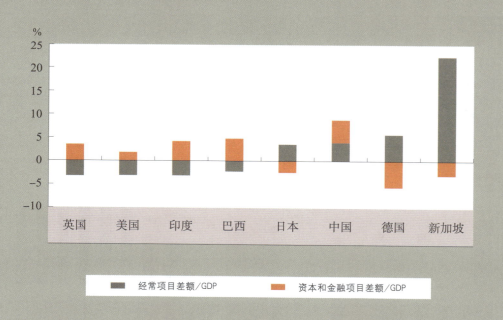

数据来源：国际货币基金组织。

键的早期预警指标[①]。否则，就容易因为资本流入（如对外借债）枯竭甚至逆转，发生本币贬值、债务危机，进而引发全面的金融经济危机。例如1994年的墨西哥、1997年的泰国和2001年的阿根廷。

过去，理论界对于经常项目顺差多少为宜没有统一标准。进入21世纪以来，随着国际社会对全球经济失衡愈演愈烈的状况日益担忧，才开始关注经常项目顺差问题。2007年，国际货币基金组织通过《对成员国汇率政策监督的决定》，要求成员国避免引发外部不稳定，包括过大的经常项目顺差。2010年底的二十国集团首尔峰会上，美国等国家曾经动议，在"均衡、强劲、可持续增长"政策框架下，各国承诺将经常项目差额控制在GDP的±4%以内。后由于各方分歧较大，会上没有达成一致，而被一揽子参考性指南所取代，且未设统一的量化标准。欧盟2011年12月出台了旨在提高经济财政一体化程度的"六项规则"，其中一项预警指标是经常项目逆差与GDP之比不应超过4%，顺差占比不应超过6%。

经常项目收支是中国对外经济交往的主要形式，也是国际收支顺差、外汇储备增长的主要来源（见表1-2和图1-11）。经常项目大额顺差是中国2005年以来才有的现象，以前是顺差和逆差交替出现且规模及占比均不大（见图1-11）。2008年以来，受周期和结构性因素的共同影响，中国经常项目顺差规模及其占GDP之比逐年下降，现已回落到国际认可的合理水平。但由于资本流出渠道不足，相关政策支持尚不到位，民间对外投资特别是金融投资水平较低，无法完全消化经常项目顺差，客观上造成国际收支"双顺差"、外汇储备继续较快增长。

[①] 参见如下文献：ⅰ. Kaminsky G., Reinhart C, "the Twin Crises: The Causes of Banking and Balance-of-Payments Problems". *The American Economic Review, June*, 1999. ⅱ. Dombusch R., "A primer on Emerging Market Crises". *Preventing Currency Crises in Emerging Markets*, University of Chicago Press, 2002. ⅲ. Mann C., "How Long the Strong Dollar?". Institute for International Economics. 2003. ⅳ. Berg A., Pattillo C., "Are Currency Crises Predictable? A Test". IMF Staff Papers, Vol. 46, No. 2. June 1999.

　　跨境资本流动波动较大。2011 年前三季度，国际通行口径的跨境资本净流入 2 500 亿美元，较 2010 年同期增长 62%。第四季度，在美欧主权债务危机影响下，国际资本避险情绪加重，跨境资金净流入套利倾向减弱，资本和金融项目转为净流出 290 亿美元（关于 2011 年第四季度我国跨境资本流动波动的讨论详见《2011 年中国跨境资金流动监测报告》）。全年，我国资本和金融项目顺差 2 211 亿美元，较上年减少 23%，与同期 GDP 之比为 3.0%，比 2010 年下降 1.8 个百分点（见表 1–2）。2011 年，我国交易引起的外汇储备由前三季度同比多增 888 亿美元转为全年少增 847 亿美元。

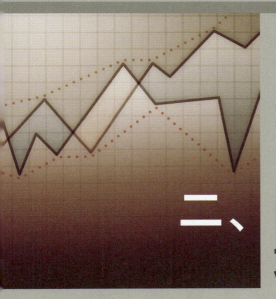

二、国际收支主要项目分析

（一）货物贸易

据海关统计，2011 年我国货物贸易呈现以下特点：

对外贸易保持较快增长，但外贸依存度较前几年明显下降。2011 年，我国进出口总额同比增加 23%，与同期 GDP 之比为 49.9%，较上年下降 0.3 个百分点，较 2006 年的历史高点回落 15.0 个百分点，显示我国经济增长的内生性进一步增强。其中，出口与 GDP 之比为 26.0%，较上年下降 0.6 个百分点，较 2006 年下降 9.7 个百分点；进口与 GDP 之比为 23.9%，较上年上升 0.3 个百分点，较 2006 年下降 5.3 个百分点（见图 2-1）。

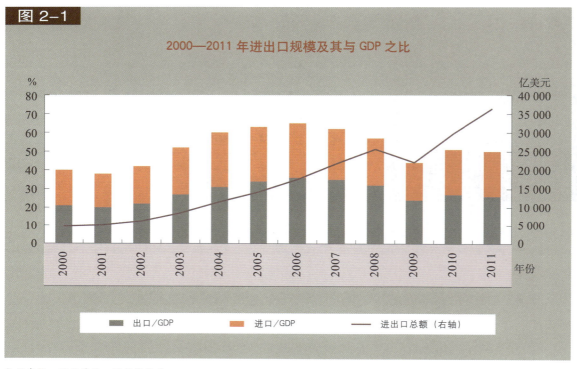

图 2-1

2000—2011 年进出口规模及其与 GDP 之比

数据来源：海关总署，国家统计局。

进口增速快于出口，进出口顺差进一步缩小。2011 年，我国出口较 2010 年增长 20%，进口增长 25%，顺差 1 551 亿美元，下降 15%。进出口顺差与同期 GDP 之比为 2.1%，较 2010 年下降 1.0 个百分点，较 2007 年的历史高点下降 5.4 个百分点（见图 2-2）。

我国对新兴市场国家进出口增长强劲，对外贸易多元化成效明显。2011 年，欧盟、美国仍为我国前两大贸易伙伴，但受欧美经济放缓的影响，其进出口总额合计占我国贸易总额的 28%，较 2010 年下降 1 个百分点。我国对东盟进出口总额较快增长，东盟超过日本成为我国对外贸易的第三大伙伴。此外，我国与巴西、俄罗斯和南非等部分新兴市场国家双边贸易发展迅速（见图 2-3）。

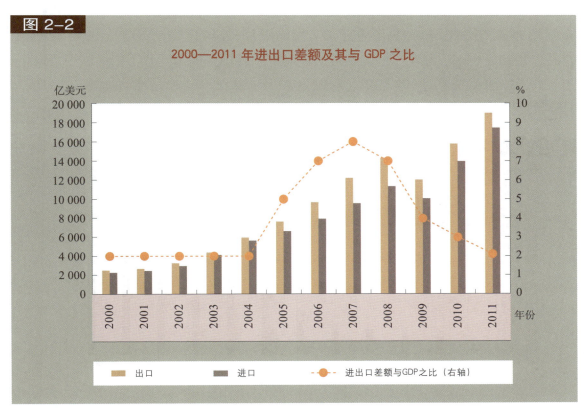

图 2-2

2000—2011 年进出口差额及其与 GDP 之比

数据来源：海关总署，国家统计局。

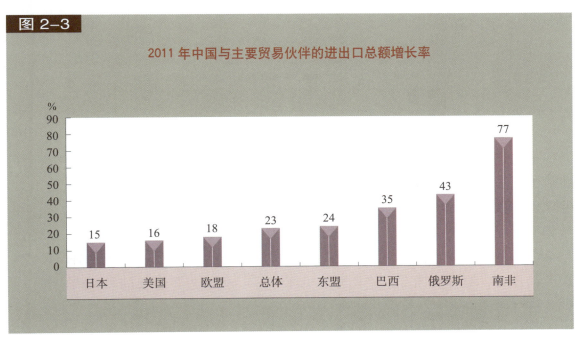

图 2-3

2011 年中国与主要贸易伙伴的进出口总额增长率

数据来源：海关总署。

加工贸易是进出口顺差的主要来源，而外商投资企业又是加工贸易顺差的主体。2011 年，我国加工贸易顺差 3 656 亿美元，较 2010 年增长 13%，同期进出口顺差总额下降 15%。其中，外商投资企业加工贸易顺差 3 144 亿美元，增长 16%，占加工贸易总顺差的 86%，显示"顺差在境内、利润归外国"的国际分工格局进一步强化。当年我国一般贸易逆差 903 亿美元，较 2010 年扩大了 91%，是推动我国进出口顺差总体收窄的重要因素（见图 2-4）。

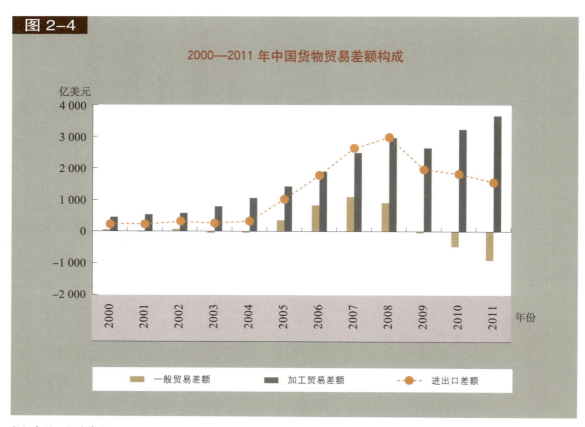

图 2-4

2000—2011 年中国货物贸易差额构成

亿美元

一般贸易差额　　　加工贸易差额　　　进出口差额

数据来源：海关总署。

进出口商品价格均较快上涨。2011 年，出口商品价格涨幅创下 2008 年金融危机以来的新高，反映了进口成本增加、劳动力价格上升和人民币汇率升值的压力。除 12 月份外，其他 11 个月，进口商品价格同比增速均快于出口，我国贸易条件指数趋于恶化（见图 2-5）。从出口增长的贡献构成看，2011 年 6 月起，出口商品价格上涨的贡献总体超过出口量增长，显示中国外贸出口面对人民币汇率升值及成本上升的压力，更多转向非价格竞争（见图 2-6）；但从进口增长的贡献构成看，主要由进口商品价格上涨拉动，反映了中国企业在国际商品市场上话语权较弱（见图 2-7）。

图 2-5

2005—2011 年进出口商品价格同比指数与贸易条件指数

贸易条件指数　　　出口价格同比指数　　　进口价格同比指数

数据来源：海关总署。

图 2-6

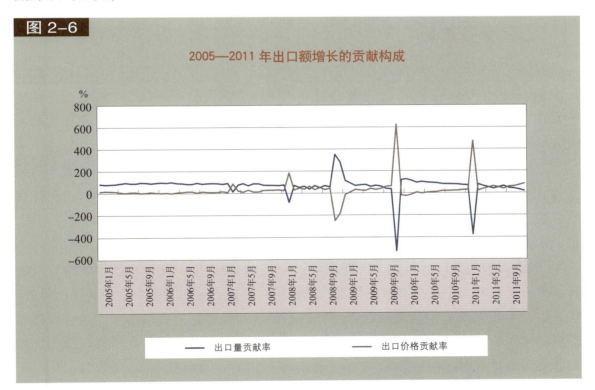

2005—2011 年出口额增长的贡献构成

出口量贡献率　　　出口价格贡献率

数据来源：海关总署。

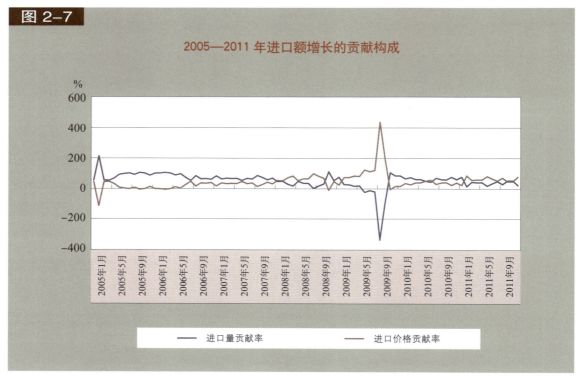

图 2-7

2005—2011 年进口额增长的贡献构成

数据来源：海关总署。

（二）服务贸易

服务贸易规模保持较快增长。按国际收支统计口径，2011 年服务贸易总额 4 209 亿美元，较上年增长 18%。服务贸易总额增速较货物贸易增速低 5 个百分点，相当于货物贸易总额的 12%，占比较上年下降 0.4 个百分点（见图 2-8）。相比发达国家服务贸易相当于货物贸易的三成到五成的水平，我国服务贸易发展潜力巨大。

运输和旅游项目逆差扩大是服务贸易逆差扩大的主要原因。2011 年，服务贸易逆差较上年增长 77%。其中，运输逆差达 449 亿美元，较上年增长 55%，占服务贸易总逆差的 81%。我国外贸进出口总量增加，境内企业对国际货物运输的需求上升，带动运输服务支出较快增长。旅游逆差达到 241 亿美元，较上年增长 1.7 倍。其中，全年我国入境旅游 1.35 亿人次，同比增长 1%，带动住宿、餐饮购物等旅游收入略长；随着国民收入水平提高，居民消费结构继续呈现多元化发展，内地居民出境 0.7 亿人次，增长 22%，带动境外观光、购物、留学等旅游支出大幅增加。从分国别和地区的情况看，内地对美国、澳大利亚、英国、加拿大和中国香港均呈现较大规模的旅游逆差（见图 2-9）。

图 2-8

2005—2011 年货物和服务贸易比较

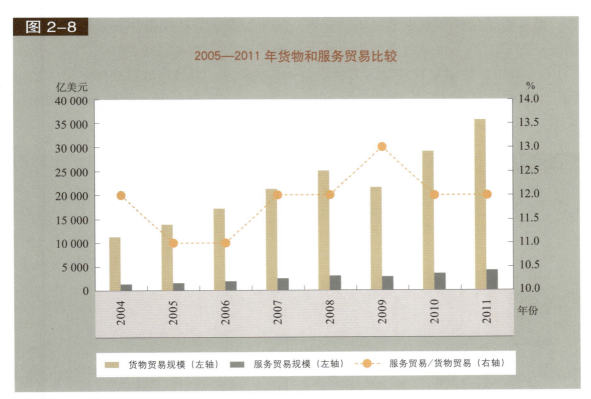

数据来源：国家外汇管理局。

图 2-9

2011 年旅游项目分国别和地区的收支情况

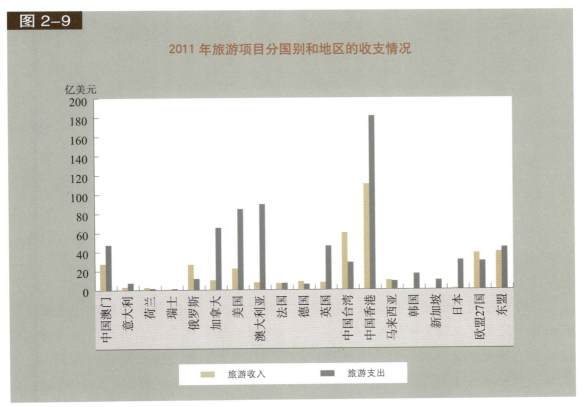

数据来源：国家外汇管理局。

服务贸易伙伴国家和地区集中度高。主要服务贸易伙伴集中在邻近地区和欧美发达国家，服务贸易收支前十名伙伴国家和地区占服务贸易总额的73%（见图2-10）。其中，我国对香港地区大幅顺差412亿美元，对台湾地区小幅顺差4亿美元，对其他主要伙伴国均呈现逆差，逆差较大的国家包括韩国、日本、澳大利亚和美国，分别为131亿美元、116亿美元、105亿美元和66亿美元。

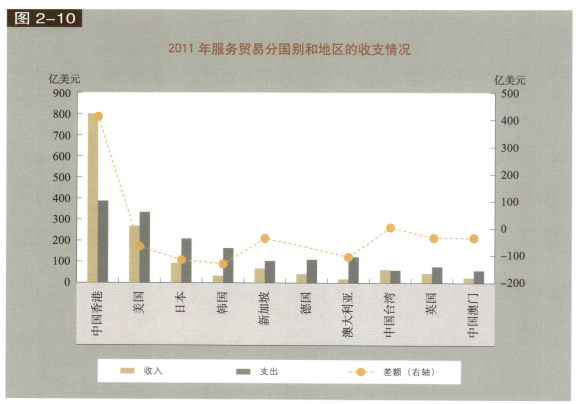

图 2-10

2011 年服务贸易分国别和地区的收支情况

数据来源：国家外汇管理局。

（三）直接投资

外国来华直接投资流入及净流入均有所下降。2011 年，外国来华直接投资流入2 543 亿美元，较上年减少4%；净流入2 201 亿美元，较上年减少10%，但仍居历史高位（见图2-11）。

对外直接投资流出保持增长，但净流出有所减少。2011 年，我国对外直接投资流出671 亿美元，较上年增加15 亿美元，创历史新高。受我国对外直接投资清盘增加和从境外关联企业收回贷款大幅增长的影响，全年对外直接投资撤资达174 亿美元，较上年增长1.3 倍，导致我国对外直接投资净流出497 亿美元，同比减少14%（见图2-12）。

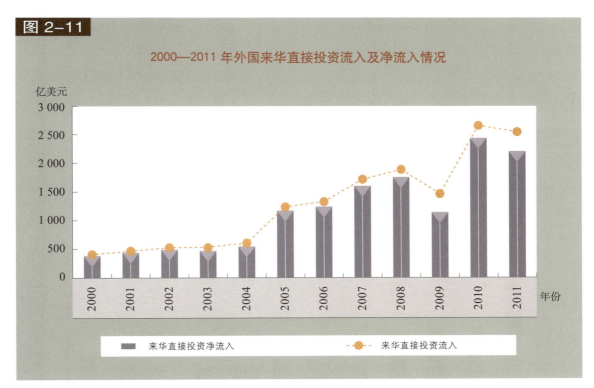

图 2-11

2000—2011 年外国来华直接投资流入及净流入情况

亿美元

图例：来华直接投资净流入 | 来华直接投资流入

数据来源：国家外汇管理局。

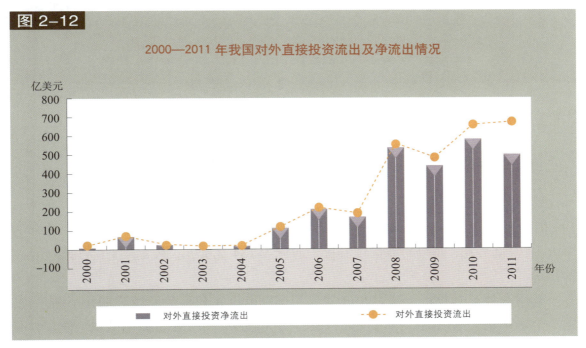

图 2-12

2000—2011 年我国对外直接投资流出及净流出情况

亿美元

图例：对外直接投资净流出 | 对外直接投资流出

数据来源：国家外汇管理局。

　　直接投资净流入是我国国际收支顺差的主要来源。2011 年，我国直接投资顺差 1 704 亿美元，较上年减少 8%（见图 2-13）。就直接投资顺差在国际收支总顺差中的占比而言，近年来总体呈现下降趋势，其他形式的资本流动对我国国际收支状况的影响加大（见图 2-13 和图 1-6）。2011 年该比重为 40%，较 2009 年的低谷回升了 24 个百分点，再次凸显金融动荡时期直接投资对于我国国际收支状况的稳定作用，同时也表明国际长期投资继续看好中国。

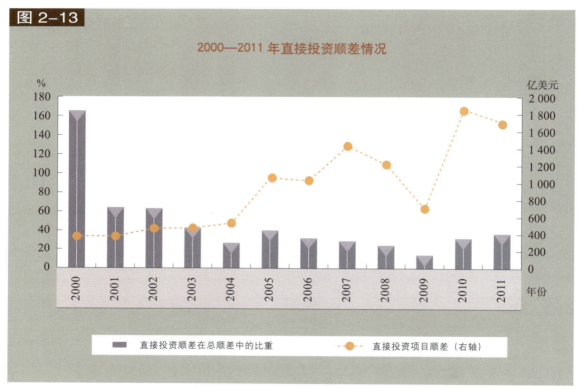

图 2-13

2000—2011 年直接投资顺差情况

图例：
- 直接投资顺差在总顺差中的比重
- 直接投资项目顺差（右轴）

数据来源：国家外汇管理局。

（四）证券投资

跨境证券投资净流入延续下降。2011 年，我国证券投资项下跨境资金净流入 196 亿美元，较上年下降 18%。其中，我国对外证券投资净流入 62 亿美元，上年为净流出 76 亿美元；境外对我国证券投资净流入 134 亿美元，较上年下降 58%（见图 2-14）。

我国对外证券投资下降。2011 年，美国和欧洲主权债务问题叠加并不断恶化，国际金融市场大幅震荡，国内投资者避险动机增强，对外投资意愿减弱。全年，我国对外股票投资新增额和撤资额分别为 101 亿美元和 112 亿美元，较上年分别下降 49% 和 2%，两项合计净流入 11 亿美元，上年为净流出 84 亿美元；我国对外债券投资新增额和撤资额分别为 91 亿美元和 143 亿美元，分别下降 37% 和 7%，两项合计净流入 51 亿美元，增长 6 倍。据国际投资头寸统计显示，截至 2011 年 9 月末，我国对外金融资产中的证券投资占比为 5.5%，略高于俄罗斯、巴西、印度等"金砖国家"，但与发达经济体差距明显（见图 2-15）。这反映出包括我国在内的新兴市场经济体受制于政策约束、市场条件等因素，民间对外金融投资渠道有限、规模不足，进而影响在国际金融市场的定价权和话语权。

境外对我国证券投资下降。在股票投资方面，2011 年全球资本市场在美欧主权债务危机冲击下遭遇寒冬，而国内企业更面临境外做空力量的持续打压，使境外上市首发和再融资规模由 2010 年的 354 亿美元大幅回落至 116 亿美元，加上合格境外机构投资者新增投资 8 亿美元，全年境外对我国股票投资净流入 53 亿美元，较上年下降 83%。在债券投资方面，2011 年境外对我国债券投资净流入 81 亿美元，较上年增长 24 倍，主要原因是 2010 年 8 月开放境外人民币清算行等三类机构运用人民币投资境内银行间债券市场所释放的政策效应，以及财政部和境内机构在香港离岸市场发行人民币债券增多。

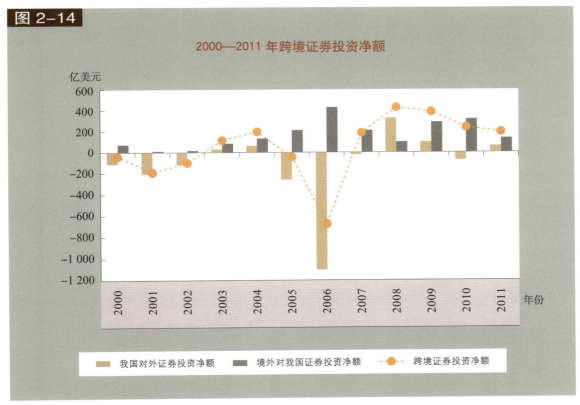

图 2-14

2000—2011 年跨境证券投资净额

注：我国对外证券投资正值表示净回流，负值表示净流出；境外对我国证券投资正值表示净流入，负值表示净流出。
数据来源：国家外汇管理局。

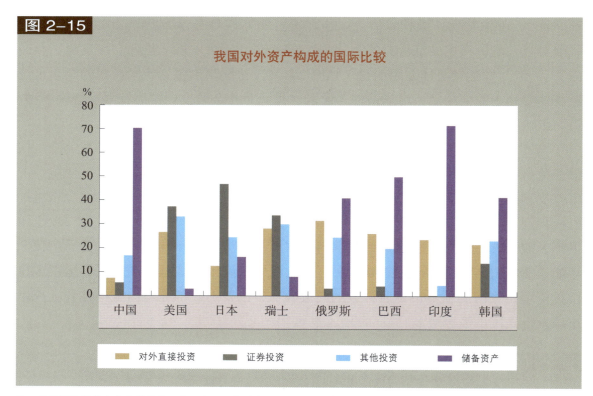

图 2-15

我国对外资产构成的国际比较

（图例）对外直接投资　证券投资　其他投资　储备资产

注：采用国际投资头寸表的统计口径。巴西、韩国为 2011 年 12 月末数据，中国、日本、印度为 2011 年 9 月末数据，美国、瑞士、俄罗斯为 2010 年 12 月末数据。
数据来源：国家外汇管理局，环亚经济数据库（CEIC），相关国家货币当局。

（五）贸易信贷

贸易信贷[①]资产负债规模持续增长（见图 2-16）。据贸易信贷抽样调查系统显示，2011 年末，贸易信贷资产余额 2 769 亿美元，较上年末增加 710 亿美元，增长 34%。其中，出口应收款 2 192 亿美元，增加 482 亿美元；进口预付款 577 亿美元，增加 228 亿美元。贸易信贷负债余额 2 492 亿美元，较上年末增加 380 亿美元，增长 18%。其中，进口应付款 1 914 亿美元，增加 434 亿美元；出口预收款 578 亿美元，减少 53 亿美元。从流量看，2011 年，我国出口应收款大幅增加而出口预收减少，显示危机环境下我国出口收账条件有所恶化。从存量看，出口应收比预收情况更突出、进口延付比预付情形更显著，这种跨境贸易融资方式难以通过流入结汇实现套利，而是基于实际贸易背景的负债美元化的财务管理运作。

[①] 贸易信贷指中国境内外企业因贸易往来而相互赊账，形成的应收／预付账款（资产方）和预收／延付账款（负债方），它反映了贸易双方占用对方资金的情况。银行提供的贸易融资和融资性担保不在此列。
贸易信贷的资产和负债方是国际收支平衡表"资本和金融项目"中"其他投资"项下的重要子项目。其中，贸易信贷的负债方也是我国外债统计的一个重要数据源，与登记外债共同构成我国外债余额。

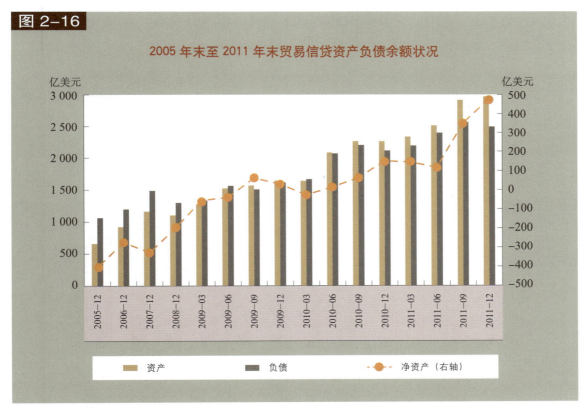

图 2-16

2005 年末至 2011 年末贸易信贷资产负债余额状况

图例：资产　负债　净资产（右轴）

数据来源：国家外汇管理局。

贸易信贷是后危机时期我国企业一种重要的融资方式。2011 年末，贸易信贷资产负债总额占当年进出口总量的比重维持在 15% 左右，较 2008 年以前有所提高（见图 2-17）。从期限看，短期贸易信贷占比较高。截至 2011 年末，样本企业短期（一年以下）贸易信贷资产占其全部资产的比重为 90%，样本企业短期贸易信贷负债占其全部负债的比重为 93%。从主体看，外商投资企业较内资企业的贸易信贷更为活跃。截至 2011 年末，就样本企业而言，外商投资企业贸易信贷资产占比为 62%，外商投资企业贸易信贷负债占比为 58%。此外，外商投资企业更多利用应收／应付进行资金安排，而内资企业更多利用预收／预付进行资金安排。

贸易信贷转为净资产，且波动较大。2011 年末，贸易信贷净资产 277 亿美元，这是我国首次成为净资产国（上年为净负债 52 亿美元）。这表明，2011 年我国企业与境外客商之间与贸易有关的资本流动总体上为净流出。其中，2011 年第一、第二季度，贸易信贷净资产显示为小幅下降（即净流入）3 亿美元和 27 亿美元，但第三、第四季度转为大幅上升（即净流出）233 亿美元和 127 亿美元（见图 2-16）。2011 年下半年贸易信贷资金由净流入转为净流出是资产增加、负债减少共同作用的结果。下半年，欧美主权债务危机逐步恶化，外部流动性紧张。受此影响，为争取海外订单，我国企业对外商业授信增多，境外企业较多占用我方贸易资金，使贸易信贷资产方增长。同时，9 月底以来，国际金融市场大幅震荡，人民币汇率打破单边升值预期，企业加速还债，使贸易信贷负债方减少。

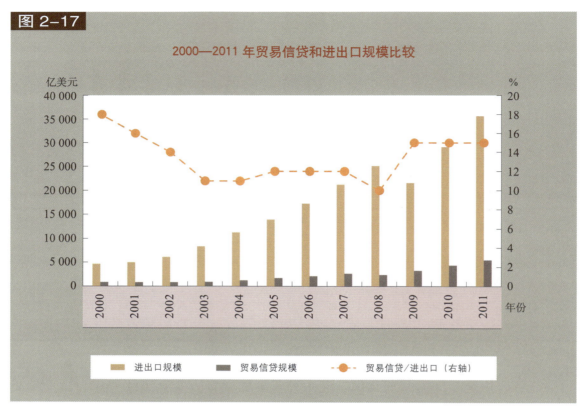

图 2-17

2000—2011 年贸易信贷和进出口规模比较

图例：进出口规模　　贸易信贷规模　　贸易信贷/进出口（右轴）

数据来源：国家外汇管理局。

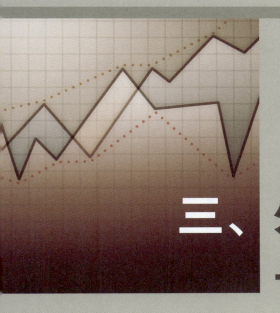

三、外汇市场运行
与人民币汇率

（一）外汇市场改革和建设情况

丰富外汇市场交易品种。在银行对客户市场和银行间外汇市场推出人民币对外汇期权业务，并适应市场需求鼓励银行为客户办理期权组合业务，促进人民币外汇衍生产品市场发展。在银行对客户市场推出人民币外汇货币掉期业务，完善货币掉期市场结构。

增加外汇市场交易币种。银行间外汇市场推出澳大利亚元和加拿大元对人民币交易，便利银行管理风险，降低跨境贸易和投资汇兑成本。

人民币外汇衍生产品市场基准体系逐步完善。银行间外汇市场相继公布外汇掉期曲线、美元隐含利率曲线、人民币隐含波动率曲线和外汇远期曲线，形成较为完整的衍生产品市场基准体系，便利了市场参与者的交易和风险管理。

（二）人民币对主要货币汇率走势

人民币对美元双边汇率继续升值。2011 年末，人民币对美元汇率中间价收于6.3009 元 / 美元，较 2010 年末升值 5.1%。2005 年人民币汇率形成机制改革以来，人民币对美元汇率中间价累计升值 31.4%（见图 3–1）。

图 3–1

2011 年人民币对美元、欧元和日元汇率中间价走势

图例：—— 美元   —— 欧元   —— 100日元

数据来源：中国外汇交易中心。

人民币汇率双向波动增强。2011 年，银行间即期外汇市场人民币对美元交易价日间最大波动（最高价 – 最低价）日均为 96 个基点，2010 年为 70 个基点；交易价相对中间价的日间最大波幅日均为 0.18%，2010 年为 0.10%。全年 244 个交易日中，交易价在 71 个交易日处于中间价升值区间波动，58 个交易日处于中间价贬值区间波动，115 个交易日围绕中间价上下波动，三个方向的分布更加平衡（见表 3–1）。9 月下旬以来，随着国内外汇供求关系的变化，银行间市场多个交易日出现交易价触及当日中间价 0.5% 的浮动区间上限（或者说人民币对美元跌停）（见图 3–2）。但交易价跌停不等于人民币汇率贬值，第四季度人民币对美元中间价升值了 0.9%。同时，在跌停价位上央行抛售外汇储备，向市场提供外汇流动性，这不同于股票跌停时有价无市的情况。

表 3–1 2006—2011 年银行间外汇市场人民币对美元即期交易价波动情况

年份	相对中间价日间最大波幅（日均）	围绕中间价上下波动	处于中间价升值区间波动	处于中间价贬值区间波动
		（交易日占比）		
2006	0.07%	83.1%	13.6%	3.3%
2007	0.11%	66.5%	25.6%	7.9%
2008	0.15%	65.4%	16.3%	18.3%
2009	0.04%	70.5%	12.3%	17.2%
2010	0.10%	61.6%	23.1%	15.3%
2011	0.18%	47.1%	29.1%	23.8%

图 3–2

2011 年银行间外汇市场人民币对美元即期交易价波动情况

最高价偏离中间价幅度   最低价偏离中间价幅度

数据来源：中国外汇交易中心。

　　人民币汇率单边预期被打破。2011 年初至 9 月中旬前,境内外均维持人民币对美元升值预期。但受世界经济复苏乏力、欧债危机持续发酵、中国经济增长放缓等内外部因素的共同影响,人民币升值预期震荡减弱,境外和境内人民币汇率预期相继在 9 月下旬和 12 月上旬由升转贬。2011 年,境内外远期市场 1 年期报价隐含的人民币升值预期幅度最高分别为 1.9% 和 3.0%,人民币贬值预期幅度最高分别为 0.6% 和 1.8%(见图 3-3 和专栏 3)。

图 3-3

2011 年境内外远期市场一年期人民币对美元升值预期

———— 银行间远期市场　　　　———— 境外NDF市场

数据来源:中国外汇交易中心,路透。

专栏 3

香港离岸人民币外汇市场的价格形成机制

　　香港离岸人民币外汇市场起步于 2004 年香港银行个人人民币兑换业务,发展于 2009 年跨境贸易人民币结算试点。依托香港作为国际金融中心的自身优势和内地金融市场的逐步开放,香港离岸市场的参与主体、交易品种和市场规模稳步增长,目前已形成即期和远期两种汇率、三条曲线 [CNH Spot(即期汇率)、CNH DF(可交割的远期汇率)、CNY NDF(不可交割的远期汇率)]。

　　一般来说，同一商品在不同市场上进行交易，如果不存在管制，套利机制将使不同市场上的价格趋同。尽管当前人民币尚未实现完全可兑换，但随着人民币跨境流动的渠道逐步增多，离岸市场与在岸市场之间已经存在自发的套利机制，使离岸价格与在岸价格之间具有内在收敛性，很难长期大幅偏离。

　　基于现阶段离岸市场与在岸市场的规模比较以及人民币有管理的浮动汇率制度，当前离岸价格的形成机制可以概括为：离岸价格以在岸价格为基础，在市场供求作用下上下波动。境外投资者和境内企业各自作为主要的人民币需求方和供给方，从不同方向影响离岸价格围绕在岸价格上下波动（见图C3-1）。

图 C3-1

影响离岸价格的市场供求因素

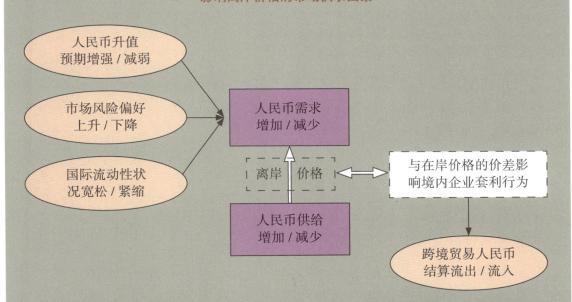

　　2011年9月下旬，香港离岸市场（CNH）即期人民币汇率相对境内市场（CNY）由溢价转为折让，价差最高达到境外1美元比境内贵0.12元人民币（即1200个基点），此后价差震荡收窄，至年末仍延续小幅折让。这体现了在欧债危机演变、做空中国等外部因素的冲击下，离岸市场投资者风险偏好、流动性及汇率预期发生较大变化，从而使离岸与在岸价格出现偏离，反过来又引发境内企业套利，使两个价格趋近的过程（见图C3-2）。

图 C3-2

2010—2011 年离岸和在岸市场人民币对美元汇率走势

| —— CNH | —— CNY | —— 中间价 |

注：CNH 和 CNY 分别代表离岸和在岸价格，均采用即期收盘价。
数据来源：中国外汇交易中心，路透。

　　在离岸价格与在岸价格之间的关系方面，有以下三个特点值得关注：

　　一是离岸价格的变化容易出现"超调"。由于在岸价格的快速变化通常被市场解读为人民币升值预期的变化，使得离岸价格在心理预期的作用下，变化速度快于在岸价格。特别地，由于离岸市场的高度开放性，使离岸人民币越来越具备像新加坡元、泰铢等亚洲货币的特性，不仅受境内市场的影响，更是全球外汇市场的一部分，在短期内可能摆脱在岸价格特别是中间价的牵制，出现大幅波动。

　　二是离岸与在岸市场发展的不同步影响两地价差。在市场参与者结构方面，随着越来越多的投资银行、对冲基金以及香港以外的参加行进入离岸市场，使人民币需求方的规模和结构发生变化，交易不再局限于初期的贸易类，非贸易类的交易比重增加并成为市场主流。更为重要的是，这种变化使得影响人民币需求的因素日益增多和复杂，增持或减持人民币已不单纯是人民币升值预期问题。在市场产品结构方面，汇率、利率等各类人民币产品的不断丰富，不仅本身可以改变离岸市场的价格形成机制，也吸引更多的参与者进入离岸市场，影响人民币供求。

三是离岸价格存在政策性的双轨制。根据现行政策安排，人民银行通过清算行为参加行提供人民币兑换窗口，但对清算行在境内银行间外汇市场买入和卖出人民币实施双向额度控制。同时，参加行在清算行办理平盘的人民币头寸仅限于贸易类交易，非贸易类交易只能进入离岸市场。这意味着，贸易和非贸易两类交易存在两种离岸价格，前者直接以在岸价格为基准，而后者还更多地受到市场供求的影响。

人民币有效汇率进一步升值。根据国际清算银行数据，2011年人民币对一篮子货币的名义有效汇率累计升值4.9%，扣除通货膨胀因素的实际有效汇率累计升值6.1%；2005年人民币汇率形成机制改革以来，人民币名义和实际有效汇率累计分别升值21.2%和30.3%（见图3-4）。在国际清算银行监测的61个经济体货币中，2011年人民币名义和实际有效汇率的升值幅度分别居第3位和第2位，俄罗斯、巴西、印度、南非等"金砖国家"货币名义和实际有效汇率平均贬值10.0%和7.4%，人民币在全球新兴市场货币中表现稳定（见专栏4）。

图 3-4

1994—2011年人民币有效汇率走势

数据来源：国际清算银行。

专栏4

2011年新兴市场经济体汇率变动及成因

2011年，新兴市场经济体汇率在外围环境变化及其自身经济和信贷周期的共同作用下，经历了前涨后跌的大幅波动。全球主要新兴市场经济体货币对美元普遍贬值，国际清算银行统计的新兴市场经济体货币多边汇率同样震荡走弱（见图C4-1）。

图 C4-1

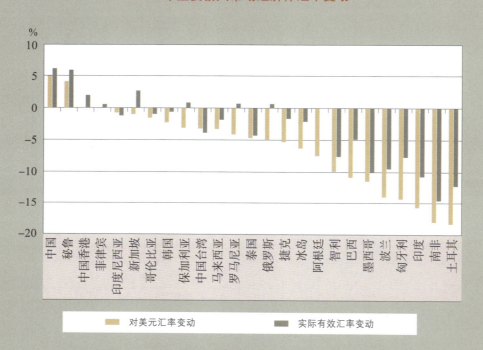

2011年主要新兴市场经济体汇率变动

数据来源：国际清算银行，彭博资讯。

跨境资本流动变化是新兴市场经济体汇率大幅波动的重要影响因素。2011年上半年，投资者对于美欧经济增长的关注超过对于欧债危机的担忧，市场信贷环境相对宽松，新兴市场基金净流入。7月末，新兴市场货币指数（EMCI）较上年末上涨3.3%。8月后，在美国债务上限问题以及欧债危机的反复冲击下，欧美银行业去杠杆化压力上升，市场信贷紧缩状况加剧，新兴市场基金转为净流出。多数新兴市场经济体货币回吐了年初以来涨幅，12月末 EMCI 指数较 7 月末下跌了 13%，较上年末下跌了 9.1%（见图 1-1）。

贸易收支状况差异使新兴市场货币走势出现分化。投资者风险偏好及资金流向变化等外部因素对贸易赤字国家的影响更为显著。对贸易赤字国而言，如果流入的资金没有有效地提升其对外贸易竞争力和相应的偿债能力，债务性资本最终会撤离。2011 年，"金砖国家"中印度和南非货币实际有效汇率全年贬值幅度均超过 10%，原因也在于投资者担心其贸易逆差的国际收支模式不可持续，将最终损及经济增长。

预计未来新兴市场汇率仍将随全球金融市场风险偏好的变化而呈现较大波动。新兴市场经济体高增长的潜力是其汇率长期走势的重要支撑因素。但从金融层面看，新兴市场经济体金融市场的深度和广度仍相对有限。截至 2011 年 6 月末，BIS 统计的 26 个主要新兴市场国家国内债券市场存量总规模仅相当于同期全球债券存量的 13.4% 和美国国债规模的 80.7%。从经济层面看，新兴市场与发达经济体实体经济的"脱钩"现象也还未出现。出口导向型新兴市场经济体汇率尤其易受外部需求变化的影响。

（三）外汇市场交易

2011 年，人民币外汇市场累计成交 8.64 万亿美元（日均成交 354 亿美元），较上年增长 26.9%。其中，银行对客户市场和银行间外汇市场分别成交 3.10 万亿美元和 5.54 万亿美元[1]（见表 3-2）。

即期外汇交易平稳增长。2011 年，银行对客户即期结售汇（不含远期履约）累计 2.7 万亿美元，较上年增长 25%；银行间即期外汇市场累计成交 3.55 万亿美元，日均成交 146 亿美元，较 2010 年日均增长 16%。2011 年，即期交易在外汇市场交易总量中的比重降至历史最低的 72%（见图 3-5），显示国内外汇市场的产品结构趋向多样化，衍生产品开始被市场主体越来越多地运用。

远期外汇交易大幅增长。2011 年，银行对客户远期结售汇累计签约 3 871 亿美元，其中结汇和售汇分别为 1 913 亿美元和 1 958 亿美元，较 2010 年分别增长 37%、16% 和 67%；银行间远期外汇市场累计成交 2 146 亿美元，日均成交 8.8 亿美元，较 2010 年日均增长 5.5 倍。

---

[1] 银行对客户市场采用客户买卖外汇总额，银行间外汇市场采用单边交易量，下同。

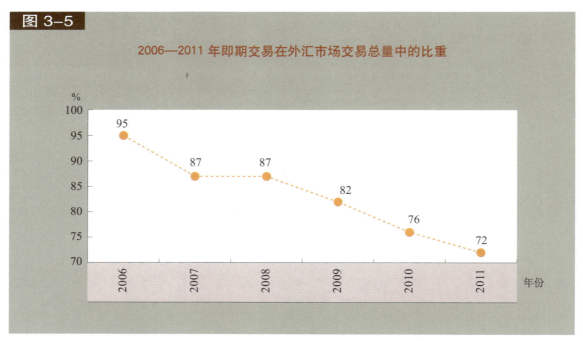

图 3-5

2006—2011 年即期交易在外汇市场交易总量中的比重

数据来源：国家外汇管理局，中国外汇交易中心。

外汇和货币掉期交易大幅增长。2011 年，银行对客户外汇和货币掉期累计签约 142 亿美元，较 2010 年增长 1.2 倍；银行间外汇和货币掉期市场累计成交 1.77 万亿美元，日均成交 72.6 亿美元，较 2010 年日均增长 37%。

外汇期权市场从无到有。2011 年 4 月 1 日，银行对客户市场和银行间外汇市场正式开展期权交易，银行间期权市场全年累计成交名义本金合计 10.1 亿美元，主要为 3 个月以内的短期限美元期权，以外汇看跌期权为主；银行对客户期权市场累计成交 8.7 亿美元，以外汇看涨期权为主。12 月末，银行间期权市场人民币对美元 3 个月和 1 年期限的隐含波动率分别为 3.23% 和 4.54%，较境外无本金交割期权市场（NDO）同期限波动率分别高出 0.1 个和 0.2 个百分点。

表 3-2　2011 年人民币外汇市场交易概况

交易品种	交易量（亿美元）
即期	62 544
银行对客户市场	27 005
银行间外汇市场	35 538
远期	6 017
银行对客户市场	3 871
银行间外汇市场	2 146
其中：3 个月（含）以下	1 282

续表

交易品种	交易量（亿美元）
3 个月至 1 年（含）	815
1 年以上	49
外汇和货币掉期	**17 853**
银行对客户市场	142
银行间外汇市场	17 710
其中：3 个月（含）以下	16 433
3 个月至 1 年（含）	1 244
1 年以上	34
期权	**19**
银行对客户市场	8.7
其中：外汇看涨／人民币看跌	8.1
外汇看跌／人民币看涨	0.6
银行间外汇市场	10.1
其中：外汇看涨／人民币看跌	2.4
外汇看跌／人民币看涨	7.7
其中：3 个月（含）以下	9.4
3 个月至 1 年（含）	0.7
1 年以上	0
合计	**86 431**
其中：银行对客户市场	31 027
银行间外汇市场	55 405
其中：即期	62 544
远期	6 017
外汇和货币掉期	17 853
期权	19

注：数据均为单边交易额，采用四舍五入原则。
数据来源：国家外汇管理局，中国外汇交易中心。

银行间外币对交易大幅增长。2011 年，9 个外币对买卖累计成交折合 947 亿美元（见表 3-3）。其中，即期交易作为最大交易品种累计成交折合 857 亿美元，日均成交 3.5 亿美元，较 2010 年日均增长 69%。银行间外币买卖市场自 2005 年推出以来，始终以美元／港币、欧元／美元两个货币对交易为主，美元／日元交易大幅萎缩，而澳元／美元交易增长较快（见图 3-6），总体上符合国际外汇市场格局和内地与香港之间特有的经济联系。

表 3-3　2011 年银行间外汇市场外币对即期交易情况

货币对	欧元/美元	澳元/美元	英镑/美元	美元/日元	美元/加元	美元/瑞士法郎	美元/港元	欧元/日元	美元/新元
成交量（亿美元）	321.3	86.4	25.6	23.0	2.5	9.9	381.4	1.3	5.3
成交量占比（%）	37.5	10.1	3.0	2.7	0.3	1.2	44.5	0.2	0.6
成交量同比增长（%）	160.7	256.6	−6.5	−31.5	−37.7	246.6	35.6	73.6	8.4
笔数	22 196	6 190	1 377	2 708	637	506	5 624	71	606

数据来源：中国外汇交易中心。

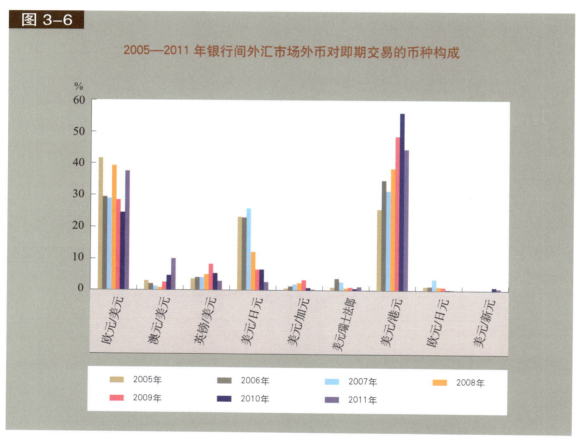

图 3-6

2005—2011 年银行间外汇市场外币对即期交易的币种构成

数据来源：中国外汇交易中心。

四、国际收支形势展望
和政策取向

（一）形势展望

2012 年，预计全球经济复苏放缓，国际资本流动不确定性依然较大。面对高企的政府债务，欧美等发达经济体将继续实施紧缩财政政策，经济增长提升空间有限。2012 年 3 月国际货币基金组织最新预计，全年全球经济增长 3.3%，较 2011 年放慢 0.5 个百分点；世界贸易总量增长 3.8%，较 2011 年下滑 3.1 个百分点。同时，美国、欧洲等主要发达经济体货币政策仍将维持宽松，全球流动性充裕的基础依然存在，但国际金融监管进一步趋严，欧债危机有可能继续向欧元区其他高负债国家蔓延，银行业风险和主权债务风险交织上升，再加上地缘政治事件等不稳定因素，全球资金避险情绪可能会有所起伏，导致跨境资本流动出现较大波动。

2012 年，我国经济将保持平稳较快发展，经济增长的内生性继续增强。虽然全年经济增长目标有所下调，但在工业化、城镇化等长期增长因素的推进下，我国经济发展前景依然向好。据国际货币基金组织最新预测，2012 年我国经济增长有望达到 8.2%，在全球范围内仍位居前列。我国经济发展的质量和效益将有所提升，通过加快经济发展方式转变和经济结构调整，内需对经济增长的作用将进一步增强，而国内物价水平也有望回落。同时，我国将进一步落实扩大消费需求、增加进口和"走出去"战略。

综上，预计 2012 年，我国国际收支仍将保持顺差，但顺差大幅减少。发达国家的结构性问题短期内难以解决，国际经济金融将持续动荡，我国可能面临跨境资本流动反复波动的风险。随着外汇供求关系趋于平衡，人民币汇率预期分化，全年人民币汇率走势可能形成有升有贬、双向波动的局面。

专栏 5

主权债务危机发展、演变与展望

2010 年以来，欧洲主权债务危机以希腊为起点在欧元区边缘国家迅速蔓延，日本和美国债务问题也引起关注。主权债务危机的发展和演变主要受以下几个因素影响并相互作用：

一是主权债务水平。从各主要国家政府总债务占 GDP 比重的横向比较看，截至 2011 年底，日本为 208.2%，希腊为 165.4%，意大利为 120.1%，美国为 99.5%。相比 2010 年底，除债务水平最高的日本有所下降外，其他国家均有不同程度的上升。居高不下的政府债务水平，增大了危机传染风险，也使主权信用评级遭受调降的可能性大幅上升。2011 年 8 月，标普调降美国评级，从 AAA 级降至 AA+ 级；希腊评级从 2009 年以来已连续调降 11 次，从 A- 级降至目前的 CC 级。

二是危机救助进展。国际货币基金组织、欧盟、欧洲中央银行等陆续出台了一系列救助措施，设法控制欧债危机继续恶化和传染风险。其中包括：建立永久性危机解决机制（ESM）并扩大可用救助资金规模；对银行业债务担保和补充资本金；对希腊等危机国家实施资金救助，并启动希腊私人投资者参与救助的计划（PSI）；等等。截至 2011 年底，已明确对危机国家救助总金额达 2 730 亿欧元，其中希腊 1 100 亿欧元，爱尔兰 850 亿欧元，葡萄牙 780 亿欧元。相关救助资金正在根据各国财政紧缩进展分批发放。

三是全球去杠杆化进程。去杠杆化是家庭、企业、银行等在危机情况下的"自救"措施。以银行业为例，去杠杆化的方式主要是控制信贷规模或出售资产以降低负债。通过去杠杆化，银行资产负债表正处于逐步恢复和重建期，但家庭和企业部门的借贷和消费水平受到了影响。

四是央行量化宽松货币政策。危机中，为刺激经济复苏，美联储承诺将零利率目标至少维持到 2014 年，并实施卖出短期国债、买入长期国债的"扭转"（twist）操作。欧洲中央银行也将基准利率维持在 1% 的水平上，通过降息、购买债券、增加流动性供给等方式放松货币政策。截至 2012 年 2 月初，欧洲中央银行购买国债规模约达 2 190 亿欧元，通过长短期再融资操作（MRO 和 LTRO）注入银行体系的资金余额约 6 170 亿欧元。英国央行量化宽松政策实施以来，国债持有量已达 2 410 亿英镑。日本央行将隔夜目标利率维持在 0.1% 的极低水平。

国际层面，二十国集团、国际货币基金组织等国际组织和全球金融合作平台正在与危机国家一起，积极探讨和寻求危机解决之道。从根本上说，全球经济稳步复苏，进而通过经济增长消化债务是走出危机的根本途径。在此之前，全球经济和金融市场不确定性仍将持续，主要发达国家的主权债务危机进程仍将曲折反复，新兴市场经济体可能面临新的冲击，全球资本流动格局的变化仍需密切关注。

（二）政策取向

2012 年，我国将继续通过加快转变经济发展方式，推进经济结构战略性调整，进一步扩大内需特别是消费需求，使经济增长转向消费、投资、出口协调拉动；在稳定出口的同时增加进口，促进对外贸易更趋平衡；在提高利用外资质量的同时加快实施"走出去"战略，放宽居民境外投资限制，采取多种措施促进国际收支状况继续改善。

外汇管理部门将把握好"稳中求进"的工作总基调，巩固和扩大应对国际金融危机冲击成果，提高外汇管理服务实体经济能力。一是坚守风险底线，构建防范跨境资本流动冲击的体制机制，密切监测跨境资金双向异常流动，完善应对预案；二是以贸易投资便利化为重点，深化贸易外汇管理改革，稳步推进资本项目可兑换，拓宽对外投资渠道；三是完善交易机制，丰富避险产品，大力发展外汇市场；四是完善外汇储备经营管理体制机制，实现储备资产安全、流动和保值增值。

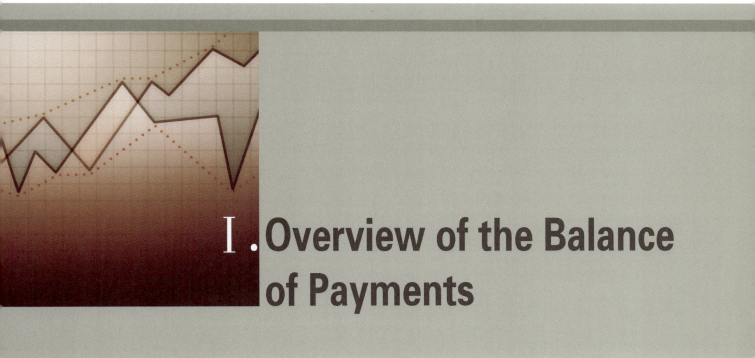

I.Overview of the Balance of Payments

(I) The balance of payments environment

In 2011 global economic growth slowed down significantly and international financial markets fluctuated dramatically. According to the latest IMF estimates, the global economic growth rate declined from 5.2 percent in 2010 to 3.8 percent in 2011. In particular, the growth rates of the major advanced economies and the emerging economies were 1.6 percent and 6.2 percent respectively, as opposed to 3.2 percent and 7.3 percent in 2010. The loose monetary policies continued, with the main task changing from anti-inflation and anti-asset bubbles to growth stimulation and financial stability (see Table 1–1). With the deteriorating sovereign debt crisis in Europe and the United States, international financial markets continued to fluctuate with increased risk aversion by investors in the second half year, and the emerging economies generally experienced capital outflows and domestic currency depreciation in contrast to the capital inflows and currency appreciation in the first half of the year (see Table 1–1; Also see the detailed discussion in Box 4).

Table 1–1   Monetary Policy Dynamics of Selected Economies, 2011

Country/Region	Monetary Policy Dynamics
Euro Zone	The refinancing benchmark was raised twice, in April and July of 2011, by 25 basis points respectively to 1.5 percent, and was cut twice in November and December by 25 basis points to 1 percent.
Australia	The benchmark interest rate was cut twice, in November and December, by 25 basis points to 4.25 percent.
Norway	In May 2011, the benchmark interest rate was raised to 2.25 percent, but in December it was cut for the first time since October 2009 by 0.5 percentage points to 1.75 percent, exceeding expectations.
China	In every month of the first half of the year, the RMB deposit reserve ratio for deposit-taking financial institutions was raised by 0.5 percentage point, on a total of six occasions to 21 percent. In February, April, and July, the benchmark interest rates for deposits and loans were raised by 25 basis points respectively. On November 30, the RMB deposit reserve ratio for deposit-taking financial institutions was cut by 0.5 percentage point.
Brazil	In March and April 2011, the SELIC overnight interest rate was raised by 50 basis points respectively and in July, it was further raised by 25 basis points to 12.5 percent. In August, October, and November, it was cut by 0.5 percentage point, on three occasions to 11 percent.
Indonesia	In February 2011, the BI interest rate was raised by 25 basis points and in October it was cut by 25 basis points. In November it was further cut by 50 basis points to 6 percent.
Thailand	In January and March, the benchmark interest rate was raised by 25 basis points respectively. In November it was cut by 25 percentage points to 3.25 percent.

In 2011 the Chinese economy developed as directed by the macro controls. The growth rate of GDP decreased slightly to 9.2 percent, down 1.2 percentage points year on year. Inflation was under preliminary control, and the CPI dropped month by month from the year high in July to 5.4 percent for the entire year (see Chart 1–2). The three driving factors behind the economic growth were coordinated: the contributions of asset formation and of final consumption were 54.2

Chart 1–1

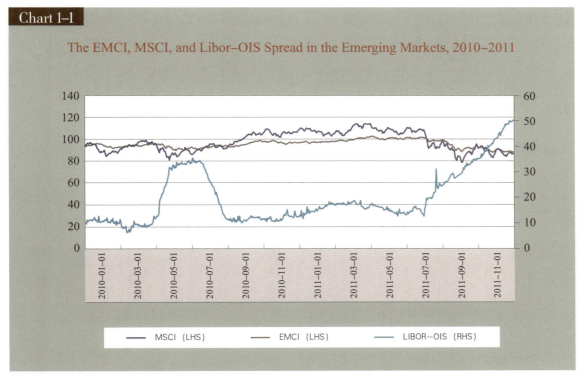

The EMCI, MSCI, and Libor–OIS Spread in the Emerging Markets, 2010–2011

Notes: January 1, 2010 was selected as the base for the MSCI and EMCI; the 3-month Libor-OIS spread reflects the credit pressures of the global banking system.

Sources: Bloomberg.

Chart 1–2

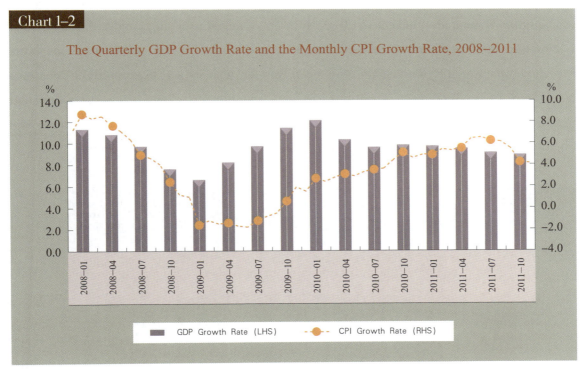

The Quarterly GDP Growth Rate and the Monthly CPI Growth Rate, 2008–2011

Sources: NBS.

Chart 1–3

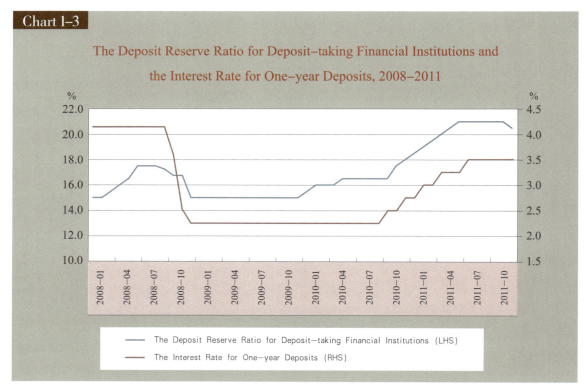

The Deposit Reserve Ratio for Deposit–taking Financial Institutions and the Interest Rate for One–year Deposits, 2008–2011

The Deposit Reserve Ratio for Deposit–taking Financial Institutions (LHS)

The Interest Rate for One–year Deposits (RHS)

Sources: PBC.

percent and 51.6 percent respectively, indicating that the contribution from domestic demand was surging as compared to that in 2010. In terms of monetary policy, under the intensified inflationary pressures, the central bank raised the deposit reserve ratio on six occasions in the first three quarters and the benchmark interest rate for deposits and loans on three occasions (see Chart 1–3); since September, the PBC has adopted a package of micro–adjustment measures to increase liquidity in the financial market and to maintain reasonable money and credit volume, including a cut in the deposit reserve ratio on November 30.

Box 1

Adjustments in External Economic Policies in 2011

In 2011 China accelerated the transformation of the mode of economic development. The policy adjustments regarding foreign trade, foreign capital utilization, and foreign exchange administration were fruitful, and the international balance of payments became more balanced. The major measures included:

Foreign trade policy was focused on maintaining stable exports and expanding imports to promote a trade balance and to upgrade construction. The rebate rates on 406 products, including steel and nonferrous metals, were eliminated to suppress the export of heavily polluting, highly energy–consuming products, resource–related products, and some agricultural products. Beginning from July 1, the tariff rate and the value–added tax on imported raw materials, including gasoline, diesel, and on imported key technical equipment, such as over–weighted oil refining equipment, natural gas pipeline and transportation equipment, were eliminated or significantly cut. During the Cannes Summit the Chinese government announced that China would guarantee a zero tariff rate for 97 percent of the products imported from the least developed countries that have foreign relations with China. China published its "Notice on the 2012 Tariff Execution Plan," clarifying that the average tariff rate for 730 products applicable for tentative import tariffs is 4.4 percent, 50 percent lower than the tariff rate applicable for most–favored nations. Moreover, the government accelerated processing trade upgrades by encouraging processing and assembly enterprises registered as legal enterprises via tax leverages. "The Outline of the 12th Five–year Plan for Trade in Services Development" was published to enhance the proportion of service trade to foreign trade.

The government focused on regulating and guiding direct investments to promote the development of both foreign capital utilization and overseas direct investments by domestic institutions. A security checking system comprised of multi government agencies for mergers and acquisitions of domestic enterprises by foreign investors was established and related regulations were implemented. The "Catalogue for the Guidence of Foreign Direct Investment Industries" was amended to encourage foreign investments in modern agriculture, services, as well as the cultural industries. In addition, the government undertook many measures, such as delegating the approval power for overseas direct investments to support overseas direct investments by domestic enterprises. Specific loans for African SME development were properly used to support direct investments in Africa by Chinese enterprises. Domestic institutions were allowed to invest abroad with RMB, and foreign investors were allowed to invest domestically with RMB. Commercial banks could extend RMB loans to overseas investment projects. Domestic financial institutions could issue RMB bonds in Hong Kong and other international financial markets.

Foreign exchange administration promotes steady and rapid economic development by facilitating trade and investment and coordinating against risks. The SAFE focused on slowing down the rapid growth in the surplus of foreign exchange sales and purchases, launched a plan to combat inflows of "hot money," and reinforced administration of foreign exchange sales and purchases, foreign exchange receipts and sales from exports, and short–term external debt. The SAFE tried to better improve inspections and focus on important cases. In 2011, 3 488 cases were examined and fined in the amount of RMB500 million, twice the amount of the fines in 2010. Thirty–nine cases of underground banks and illegal foreign exchange transactions were uncovered, with a total amount of RMB 71.7 billion. In 2011, the Pilot Reform on Verifications of Foreign Exchange Payments for Imports was smoothly carried out to reduce financial costs for enterprises and banks. The program for overseas deposits of export revenue was extended throughout the country to facilitate the holding of foreign exchange. Approval power for five categories of transactions, for example, trade credit registrations and external guarantees, was delegated to the SAFE branches. Foreign exchange sales and purchases via electronic banking by individuals were facilitated. The pilot program on RQFII was carried out to promote the opening of the capital market. The government guided foreign exchange product innovation and development by introducing RMB–Against–Foreign Exchange Options Trading to reduce foreign exchange risk aversion by market participants.

(II) Main Characteristics of the Balance of Payments

China's BOP posted decreased amounts of twin surpluses. In 2011 China's current account posted a surplus of USD 201.7 billion, down 15 percent year on year. The capital and financial account surplus totaled USD 221.1 billion, down 23 percent year on year.[1] The total BOP surplus was USD 422.8 billion, decreasing 19 percent year on year and less than the amount of the average surplus of USD 468.6 billion during the 2007–2010 period (see Table 1–2).

---

[1] The SAFE adjusted the BOP statistics according to the latest data in its joint annual survey on foreign–funded enterprises regarding unpaid and unremitted profits of foreign shareholders. Before the adjustment, the SAFE estimated the unpaid and unremitted profits by assuming a profit rate for foreign–funded enterprises during the 2007–2009 period that was lower than that indicated by the data in the joint survey.

Table 1–2   Structure of the BOP Surplus, 2005–2011

Unit: USD 100 mn

Item	2005	2006	2007	2008	2009	2010	2011
BOP surplus	235.1	285.4	449.1	458.7	442.0	524.7	422.8
Current Account surplus	134.1	232.7	354.0	412.4	261.1	237.8	201.7
As of BOP surplus (%)	57.0	81.5	78.8	89.9	59.1	45.3	47.7
As of GDP (%)	5.9	8.6	10.1	9.1	5.2	4.0	2.8
Capital and financial account surplus	101.0	52.6	95.1	46.3	180.8	286.9	221.1
As of BOP surplus (%)	43.0	18.4	21.2	10.1	40.9	54.7	52.3
As of GDP (%)	4.5	1.9	2.7	1.0	3.6	4.8	3.0

Sources: SAFE; NBS.

The surplus in trade in goods decreased slightly. Based on the balance of payments statistics, goods exports and imports amounted to USD 1 903.8 billion and USD 1 660.3 billion respectively, up by 20 percent and 25 percent, resulting a trade in goods surplus of USD 243.5 billion, down by 4 percent[①] (see Chart 1–4).

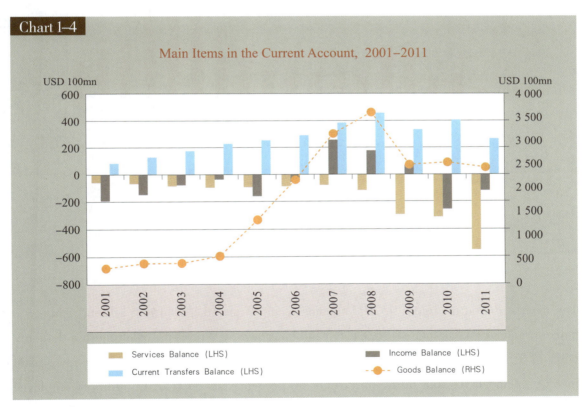

Chart 1–4

Main Items in the Current Account, 2001–2011

Sources: SAFE.

---

① The BOP statistics and the statistics of the General Administration of Customs regarding trade in goods can be reconciled by the following. First, the imports based on the BOP statistics equal 95 percent of the imports based on the custom statistics by quoting the CIF and assuming 5 percent to be insurance and freight. Second, the BOP statistics include goods repatriation, goods purchased at ports, and smuggled goods which were deducted from the import and export returns.

The deficit in trade in services grew significantly. In 2011 revenue from trade in services amounted to USD 182.8 billion, a rise of 13 percent year on year, with payments of USD 238.1 billion, up by 23 percent year on year, leading to a total deficit of USD 55.2 billion, an increase by 77 percent. The surplus of trade in goods and services totaled USD 188.3 billion, 16 percent lower than that in the previous year, and its ratio to GDP was 2.6 percent, following the declining trend since 2007 (see Chart 1–5).

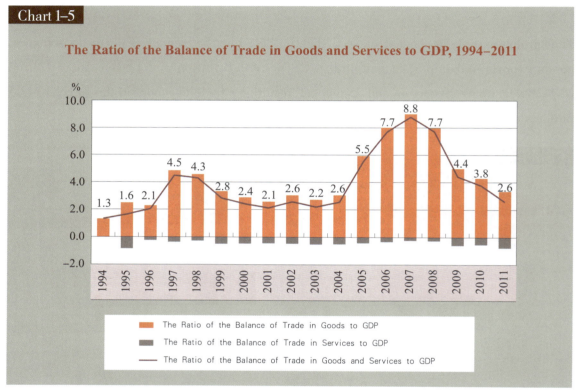

Chart 1–5

The Ratio of the Balance of Trade in Goods and Services to GDP, 1994–2011

Sources: SAFE.

The income deficit declined. In 2011 income receipts totaled USD 144.6 billion, rising by 2 percent, and payments totaled USD 156.5 billion, down by 7 percent, resulting in a deficit of USD 11.9 billion, a drop of 54 percent year on year. In particular, the deficit in investment income totaled USD 26.8 billion, a drop of 30 percent year on year. In addition, employee compensation recorded a net inflow of USD 15 billion, up by 23 percent year on year.

The surplus in direct investment decreased. In 2011 the surplus in direct investment was USD 170.4 billion, a decrease of 8 percent year on year. In particular, net inflows of inward foreign direct investment totaled USD 220.1 billion, a decrease of 10 percent. And net outflows of outward direct investment totaled USD 49.7 billion, a decrease of 14 percent (see Chart 1–6).

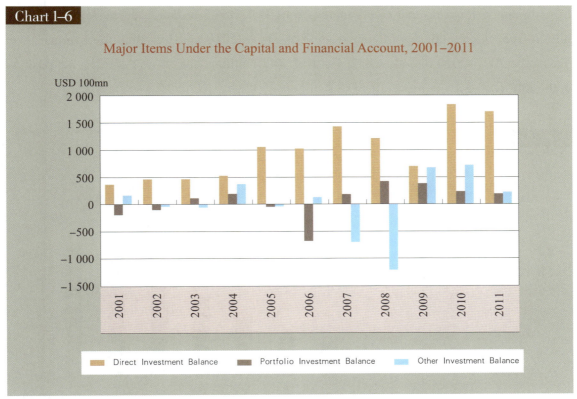

Chart 1–6

Major Items Under the Capital and Financial Account, 2001–2011

USD 100mn

Legend: Direct Investment Balance   Portfolio Investment Balance   Other Investment Balance

Sources: SAFE.

Net inflows of portfolio investment dropped rapidly. In 2011 net inflows of portfolio investment totaled USD 19.6 billion, a decrease of 18 percent year on year. In particular, net inflows of outward portfolio investment totaled USD 6.2 billion, whereas in 2010 they posted a net outflow of USD 7.6 billion. Inward portfolio investment recorded a net inflow of USD 13.4 billion, a decrease of 58 percent.

Net inflows of other investments decreased significantly. In 2011 other investments recorded a net inflow of USD 25.5 billion, a decrease of 65 percent year on year. In particular, due to increased loans extended by domestic enterprises and banks and overseas deposits, other investment assets increased by USD 166.8 billion, up 43 percent year on year; and debt borrowed by domestic enterprises and banks from abroad and deposits in domestic banks by nonresidents increased, leading to an increase of USD 192.3 billion in other investment liabilities, 2 percent more than that in the previous year.

The growth of reserve assets decelerated. In 2011 China's international reserves grew by USD 387.8 billion, excluding valuation factors such as the exchange rate and asset prices. In particular, foreign reserve assets increased by USD 384.8 billion, a decrease of USD 84.7 billion from the cumulative foreign reserve assets in 2010 and less than the average level during the 2007–2010 period , which was USD 447.7 billion (see Chart 1–7). The net position in the IMF posted an increase of USD 3.4 billion.

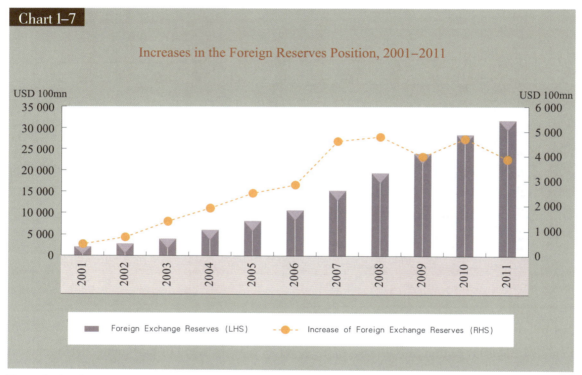

Chart 1–7

Increases in the Foreign Reserves Position, 2001–2011

Notes: The chart indicates the growth of foreign reserves due to transactions and excludes valuation factors.
Sources: SAFE.

Net errors and omissions posted a negative position. In 2011 net errors and omissions posted a net position of USD 35 billion in the debit column, accounting for −1 percent of total exports and imports of goods, far less than the international standard of ± 5% (see Chart 1–8). Net errors and omissions are caused by multi statistical sources because the coverage, timing, and valuation standards in the different sources of data vary. Since 2001, net errors and omissions posted a net position on the debit side for 5 years and on the credit side for 6 years, indicating that this is not necessarily related to "hot money" (see Box 2 in "China's Balance of Payments Report for the First Half of 2005" for a detailed discussion).

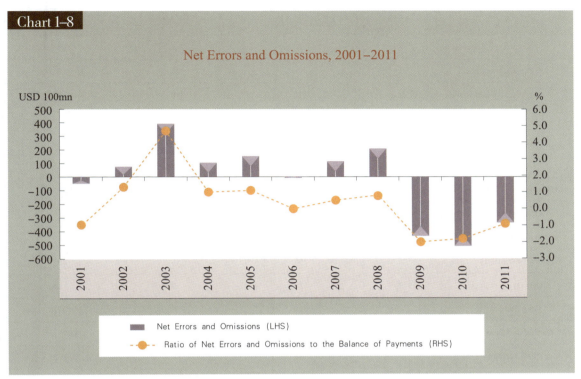

Chart 1–8

Net Errors and Omissions, 2001–2011

Sources: SAFE.

Table 1–3   China's Balance of Payments Statement in 2011①

Unit: USD 100 million

Item	Balance	Credit	Debit
I. Current account	**2 017**	**22 868**	**20 851**
A. Goods and services	**1 883**	**20 867**	**18 983**
a. Goods	**2 435**	**19 038**	**16 603**
b. Services	**−552**	**1 828**	**2 381**
1. Transportation	−449	356	804
2. Travel	−241	485	726
3. Communication services	5	17	12
4. Construction services	110	147	37
5. Insurance services	−167	30	197
6. Financial services	1	8	7
7. Computer and information services	83	122	38

① China's balance of payments statement is compiled in accordance with the principles of the fifth edition of the *Balance of Payments Manual* of the International Monetary Fund, recording all economic transactions between residents of the Chinese mainland (excluding residents of Hong Kong SAR, Macau SAR, and Taiwan province) and non-residents based on the principle of a double-entry system.

(continued)

Item	Balance	Credit	Debit
8. Royalties and licensing fees	−140	7	147
9. Consulting services	98	284	186
10. Advertising and public opinion polling	12	40	28
11. Audio-visual and related services	−3	1	4
12.Other business services	140	323	183
13. Government services, n.i.e.	−3	8	11
B. Income	**−119**	**1 446**	**1 565**
1.Compensation of employees	150	166	16
2.Investment income	−268	1 280	1 549
C. Current transfers	**253**	**556**	**303**
1.General government	−26	0	26
2. Other sectors	278	556	277
II. Capital and financial account	**2 211**	**13 982**	**11 772**
A. Capital account	**54**	**56**	**2**
B. Financial account	**2 156**	**13 926**	**11 770**
1. Direct investment	**1 704**	**2 717**	**1 012**
1.1 Abroad	−497	174	671
1.2 In China	2 201	2 543	341
2. Portfolio investment	**196**	**519**	**323**
2.1 Assets	62	255	192
2.1.1 Equity securities	11	112	101
2.1.2 Debt securities	51	143	91
2.1.2.1 Bonds and notes	50	137	88
2.1.2.2 Money market instruments	2	5	4
2.2 Liabilities	134	265	131
2.2.1 Equity securities	53	152	99
2.2.2 Debt securities	81	113	32
2.2.2.1 Bonds and notes	30	61	32
2.2.2.2 Money market instruments	51	51	0
3. Other investment	**255**	**10 690**	**10 435**
3.1 Assets	−1 668	1 088	2 756
3.1.1 Trade credits	−710	0	710
Long-term	−14	0	14

(continued)

Item	Balance	Credit	Debit
Short-term	−695	0	695
3.1.2 Loans	−453	61	513
Long-term	−433	8	441
Short-term	−20	53	73
3.1.3 Currency and deposits	−987	501	1 489
3.1.4 Other assets	482	526	44
Long-term	0	0	0
Short-term	482	526	44
3.2 Liabilities	1 923	9 602	7 679
3.2.1 Trade credits	380	454	74
Long-term	6	8	1
Short-term	374	447	73
3.2.2 Loans	1 051	7 343	6 292
Long-term	130	538	408
Short-term	920	6 805	5 884
3.2.3 Currency and deposits	483	1 719	1 237
3.2.4 Other liabilities	10	86	76
Long-term	−15	24	39
Short-term	24	61	37
III. Reserve assets	**−3 878**	**10**	**3 888**
1. Monetary gold	0	0	0
2. Special drawing rights	5	5	0
3. Reserve position in the fund	−34	6	40
4. Foreign exchange	−3 848	0	3 848
5. Other claims	0	0	0
IV. Net errors and omissions	**−350**	**0**	**350**

(Ⅲ) Evaluation of the Balance of Payments

In 2011 China's external economic activity maintained rapid growth. Balance of payments transactions totaled USD 6.95 trillion, up by 22 percent year on year and recording a historical high. The ratio to GDP was 95 percent, 0.6 percentage points lower than that in 2010 (see Chart 1–9).

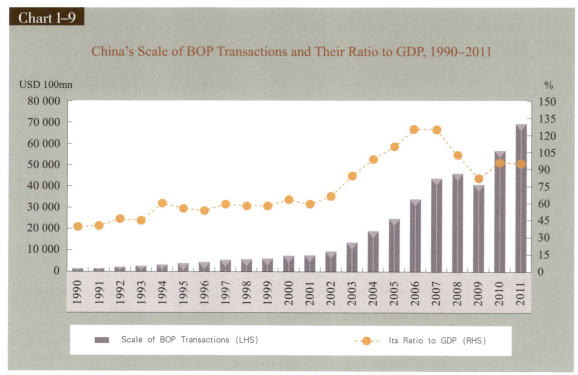

Chart 1-9

China's Scale of BOP Transactions and Their Ratio to GDP, 1990-2011

USD 100mn

%

Scale of BOP Transactions (LHS)

Its Ratio to GDP (RHS)

Sources: SAFE; NBS.

Cross-border capital flows tended to be more active. In 2011 capital and financial account transactions amounted to USD 2.58 trillion, accounting for 37 percent of the BOP transactions (see Chart 1-10), and current account transactions totaled USD 4.37 trillion, accounting for 63 percent of the BOP transactions, 26 percentage points higher than the ratio of the capital and financial account. The difference between the current account and the capital and financial account to the total BOP transactions was narrowed by 32 percentage points compared to that in 2001. In 2011 the capital and financial account surplus accounted for 52 percent of the total surplus and continued to be the top source of accumulation of foreign reserves for the second successive year (see Table 1-2).

The balance in the current account was further improved. In 2011 the current account surplus decreased by 15 percent year on year and its ratio to GDP was 2.8 percent, down 1.2 percentage points (see Chart 1-11). Based on international standards, since 2008 the ratio of the current account surplus to GDP has declined to a reasonable level (see Box 2), indicating that the transformation of the mode of economic development and external economic policy adjustments have been successful. In addition, it reflects the changed financial situations both domestically and abroad, and the more reasonable RMB exchange rate.

Chart 1–10

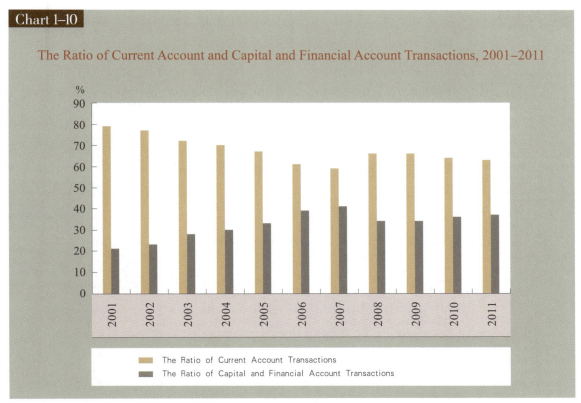

The Ratio of Current Account and Capital and Financial Account Transactions, 2001–2011

Sources: SAFE; NBS.

Chart 1–11

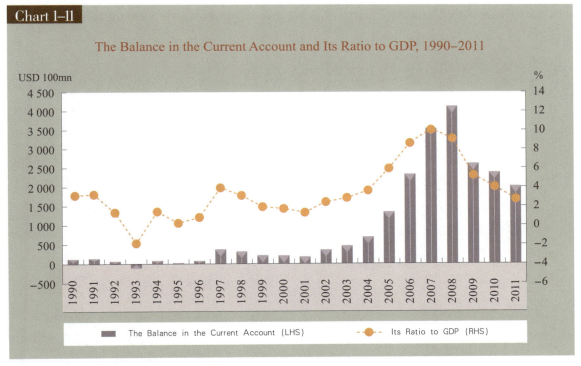

The Balance in the Current Account and Its Ratio to GDP, 1990–2011

Sources: General Administration of Customs; NBS.

Box 2

How to Evaluate the BOP Situation

The balance of payments, also referred to as the external equilibrium, is one of the four targets of macroeconomic policy. In open economies, the domestic equilibrium and the external equilibrium are closely related to reciprocal influences. Deviations from a domestic equilibrium, including growth, employment, and prices, will be reflected as a deviation from the external balance. Without an external balance, it is impossible for an economy to sufficiently allocate resources in both the domestic and international markets to realize better employment and to promote economic and social development.

In reality, the sustainability of the current account balance is regarded as a major standard for evaluating the external equilibrium. In an economy with an open capital account, the capital account plays a role in the sterilization of the current account, which means that capital flows in when the current account posts a deficit and flows out when the current account posts a surplus (see Chart C2–1). A lesson drawn from many BOP crises is that the ratio of the current account deficit to GDP is a key early warning indicator, with a threshold standing at 4–5 percent.[1] A currency devaluation as well as a debt crisis, or even an overall financial and economic crisis, might be triggered by a sudden stop in capital inflows and even capital outflows. The Mexican crisis in 1994, the crisis in Thailand in 1997, and the crisis in Argentina in 2001 are examples.

In past theoretical discussions there was no agreement on a proper level for the current account surplus. Since the beginning of the new century, more concerns about the current account surplus were raised due to the deteriorating international imbalances. In 2007 the IMF decided to place the exchange rate policies of member countries under surveillance, urging member countries not to cause external instabilities due to excessive current account surpluses. During the G20 Seoul Summit held at the end of 2010, some countries including the United States proposed that the G20 countries should commit to a threshold of ± 4 percent with respect to the ratio of the balance in the current account to GDP under

---

① G. Kaminsky and C. Reinhart, "The Twin Crises: The Causes of Banking and Balance–of–Payments Problems," *American Economic Review,* Vol. 89, No. 3, June, 1999; R. Dombusch, "A Primer on Emerging Market Crises," *Preventing Currency Crises in Emerging Markets,* University of Chicago Press, 2002; C. Mann, "How Long the Strong Dollar?" Institute for International Economics, 2003; A. Berg and C. Pattillo, "Are Currency Crises Predictable? A Test," *IMF Staff Paper,* Vol. 46, No. 2, June, 1999.

the policy framework of balanced, strong, and sustainable growth. However, this was replaced by a guidance package and no uniform quantitative standards were set because of significant differences among the countries. In December 2011, the European Union introduced six rules to promote economic and fiscal integrity; one of the indicators is the ratio of the current account deficit to GDP, which should be less than 4 percent for deficits and 6 percent for surpluses.

Chart C2–1

The Ratio of the Balances in the Current and Capital Accounts to GDP, 2010

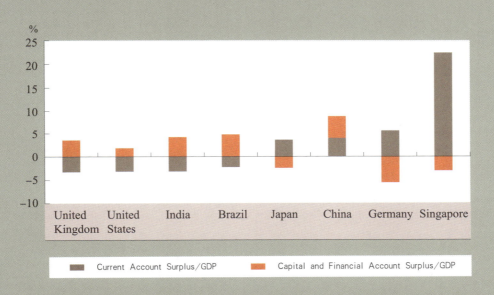

Current Account Surplus/GDP   Capital and Financial Account Surplus/GDP

Sources: IMF.

In China, the current account constitutes the main part of external economic activities and is the major source of the BOP balance as well as of the accumulation of foreign reserves (see Table 1–2 and Chart 1–11). Since 2005 there has been a large current account surplus. Prior to 2005, the current account alternately posted relatively small–scale surpluses and deficits (see Chart 1–11). Influenced by periodic and structural factors, since 2008 the ratio of the current account surplus to GDP has fallen year by year to a reasonable level. However, due to insufficient channels for capital outflows and policy support, outward investments, especially financial investments, are still too low to absorb the current account surplus and result in a twin surplus and rapid growth of foreign reserves.

Cross–border capital flows fluctuated. In the first three quarters, cross–border capital inflows totaled USD 250 billion, up by 62 percent year on year. In the fourth quarter, risk aversion in international markets worsened due to the sovereign debt crisis in the United States and Europe, causing a weakened arbitrage inclination for capital inflows, and China recorded a net outflow of USD 29 billion (see the detailed discussion on capital flow movements in 2011Q4 in "The Cross–border Capital Flow Report of 2011"). For the whole year, China recorded a capital and financial account surplus of USD 221.1 billion, down by 23 percent year on year and its ratio to GDP was 3 percent, down by 1.8 percentage points (see Table 1–2). In 2011 growth of foreign reserve transactions totaled USD 84.7 billion less than that in the previous year, but USD 88.8 billion more than that in the first three quarters.

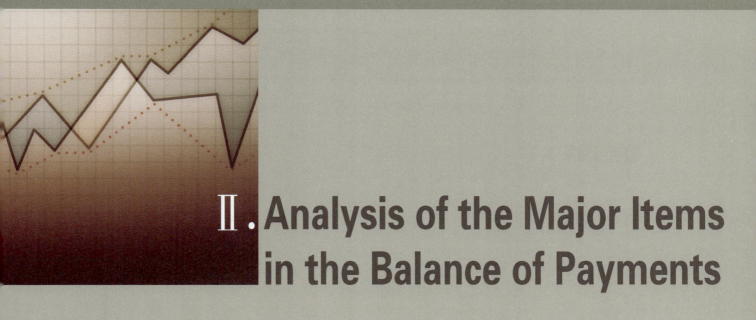

II. Analysis of the Major Items
in the Balance of Payments

(I) Trade in goods

According to the statistics of the General Administration of Customs, China's trade in goods showed the following characteristics in 2011:

Foreign trade maintained rapid growth with declining foreign trade dependency. In 2011 the volume of foreign trade grew by 23 percent year on year, and its ratio to GDP was 49.9 percent, down 0.3 percentage point year on year and down 15 percentage points from the historical high in 2006, indicating increased endogenous growth. In particular, the ratio of exports to GDP was 26 percent, down 0.6 percentage point year on year and down 9.7 percentage points from that in 2006; and the ratio of imports to GDP was 23.9 percent, up 0.3 percentage point year on year but down 5.3 percentage points from that in 2006 (see Chart 2–1).

Chart 2–1

The Ratio of Foreign Trade to GDP, 2000–2011

- The ratio of exports to GDP
- The ratio of imports to GDP
- The volume of foreign trade

Sources: General Administration of Customs; NBS.

Imports grew faster than exports, and the trade surplus declined. In 2011 China's exports increased by 20 percent year on year and imports increased by 25 percent, resulting in a surplus of USD 155.1 billion, down by 15 percent. The ratio of the trade surplus to GDP was 2.1 percent, down by 1 percentage point year on year and 5.4 percentage points lower than the historical high in 2007 (see Chart 2–2).

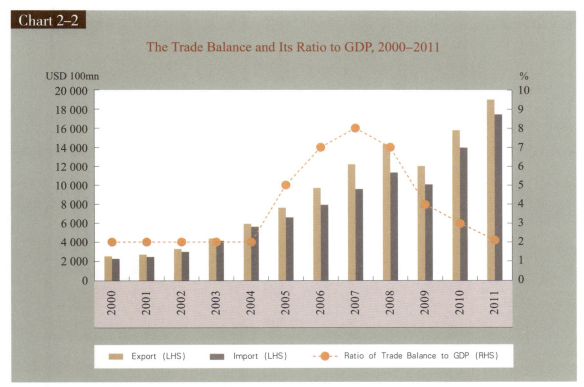

Chart 2-2

The Trade Balance and Its Ratio to GDP, 2000–2011

USD 100mn

%

Export (LHS)　　Import (LHS)　　Ratio of Trade Balance to GDP (RHS)

Sources: General Administration of Customs; NBS.

China's trade diversification was greatly improved, with strong growth of trade with the emerging markets. In 2011 the European Union and the United States were China's top two trading partners. However, due to slow economic growth, trade with the European Union and the United States accounted for 28 percent of China's total foreign trade, decreasing by 1 percentage point year on year. Trade with the ASEAN grew rapidly, becoming China's third biggest trading partner in place of Japan. In addition, bilateral trade with the emerging markets, such as Brazil, Russia, and South Africa, developed rapidly.

Processing trade was the main source of the trade surplus and foreign–funded enterprises were the main contributors. In 2011 the processing trade surplus totaled USD 365.6 billion, increasing by 13 percent year on year, while the total foreign trade surplus decreased by 15 percent. In particular, processing trade by foreign–funded enterprises was USD 314.4 billion, growing by 16 percent and accounting for 86 percent of the total processing trade surplus. This indicates that the international division of labor with surplus foreign profits was further strengthened. In 2011 ordinary trade recorded a deficit of USD 90.3 billion, expanding by 91 percent year on year and serving as the main factor in the cutting of the trade surplus.

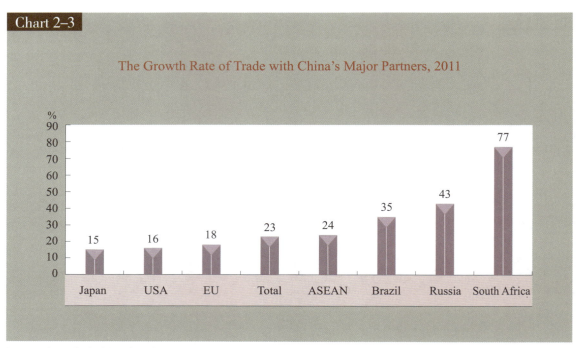

Sources: General Administration of Customs.

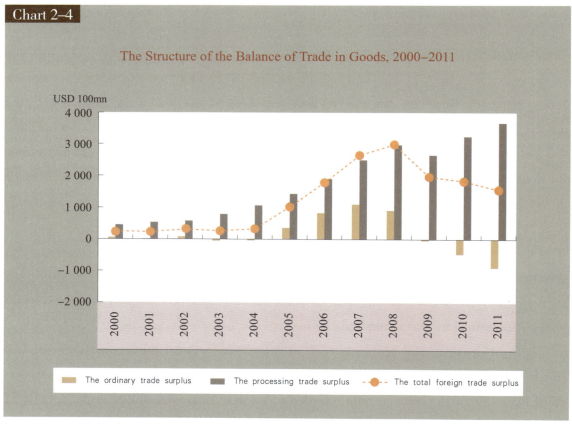

Sources: General Administration of Customs.

Chart 2–5

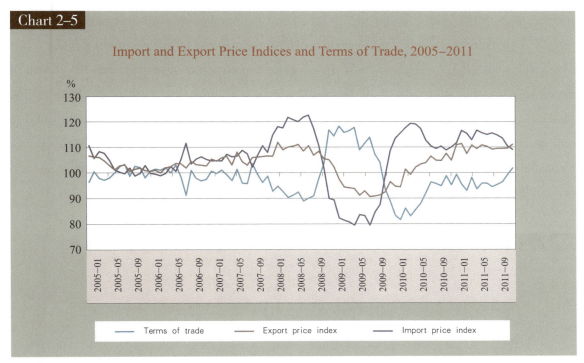

Sources: General Administration of Customs.

Chart 2–6

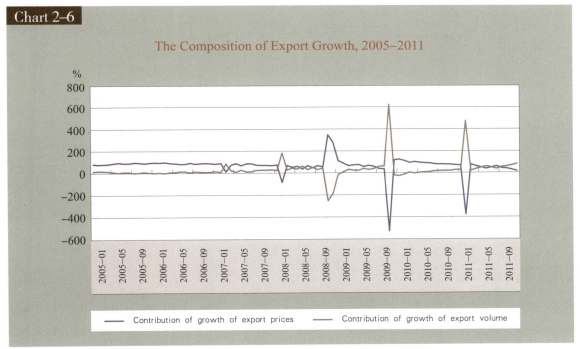

Sources: General Administration of Customs.

The prices of imports and exports surged significantly. In 2011 export prices recorded a historical high since the 2008 financial crisis, reflecting the increased costs of imports and pressures from the appreciation in the labor and exchange rate. Import prices grew more rapidly than export prices during 11 months (with the exception of in December) and the terms of trade deteriorated (see Chart 2–5). In terms of the structure of export growth, growth of export prices contributed more than the growth of export volume since June of 2011, indicating that China was facing the increased costs of currency appreciation and enterprises turned to non–price competition (see Chart 2–6). In terms of the structure of import growth, import prices were the main contributors, reflecting the weak power of Chinese enterprises in international commodity markets (see Chart 2–7).

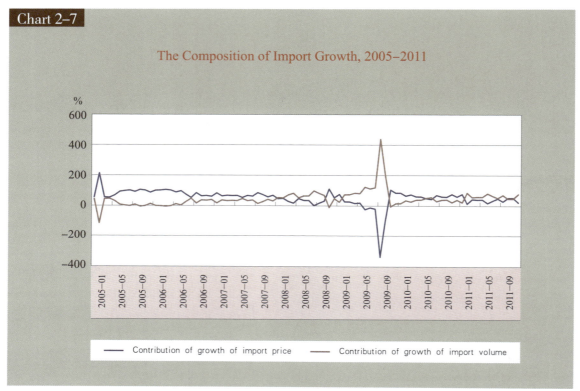

Chart 2–7

The Composition of Import Growth, 2005–2011

—— Contribution of growth of import price   —— Contribution of growth of import volume

Sources: General Administration of Customs.

(II) Trade in Services

Trade in services grew rapidly. Based on the balance of payments statistics, in 2011 trade in services totaled USD 420.9 billion, growing by 18 percent year on year, which was 5 percentage points lower than the growth of trade in goods and accounted for 12 percent of the trade in goods, down 0.4 percentage point year on year (see Chart 2–8). Compared with the developed countries where trade in services normally accounts for 30–50 percent of trade in goods, the development potential of trade of China's services is huge.

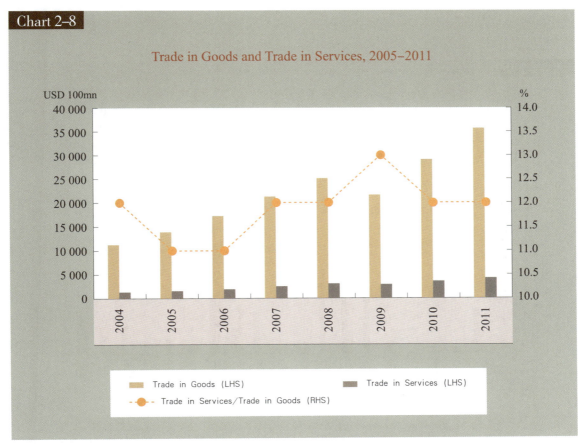

Chart 2–8

Trade in Goods and Trade in Services, 2005–2011

Sources: SAFE.

The deficit in trade and services expanded because of growth in the transportation and travel deficit. In 2011 the trade in services deficit increased by 77 percent year on year. In particular, the transportation deficit totaled USD 44.9 billion, up 55 percent year on year and accounting for 81 percent of the total trade in services deficit. Transportation payments recorded rapid growth due to the rising demand for international cargo transportation by domestic enterprises because of the growing foreign trade. The travel deficit amounted to USD 24.1 billion, 1.7 times the deficit in 2010. In particular, the number of to China totaled 135 million, increasing by 1 percent year on year and driving up the growth of travel revenue, such as accommodations, restaurants, and shopping. Resident consumption diversified with improved household income. In 2011 there were 70 million outbound visitors, up 22 percent year on year, driving significant growth in travel payments, shopping, and study. In terms of countries and regions, the travel deficit to the United States, Australia, Great Britain, Canada, and Hong Kong SAR posted a large deficit (see Chart 2–9).

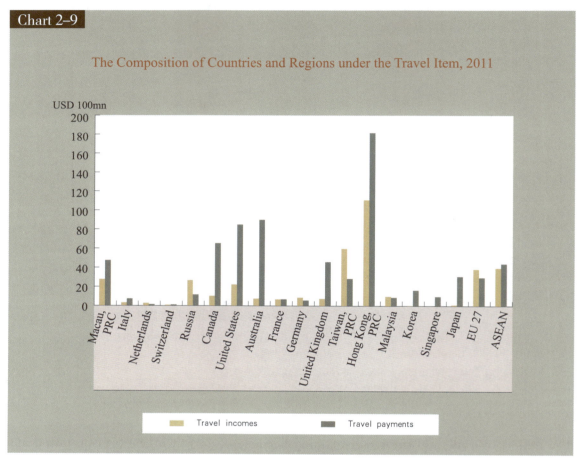

Chart 2–9

The Composition of Countries and Regions under the Travel Item, 2011

Sources: SAFE.

Partners for trade in services were highly concentrated. Major trading partners were neighboring countries and developed countries in Europe and the United States; the top ten trading partners accounted for 73 percent of the total trade in services (see Chart 2–10). In particular, trade with Hong Kong SAR recorded a surplus of USD 41.2 billion, trade with Taiwan Province posted a small surplus of USD 400 million, and trade with other trading partners posted a deficit. The major deficit partners included Korea, Japan, Australia, and the United States, with deficits of USD 13.1 billion, USD 11.6 billion, USD 10.5 billion, and USD 6.6 billion respectively.

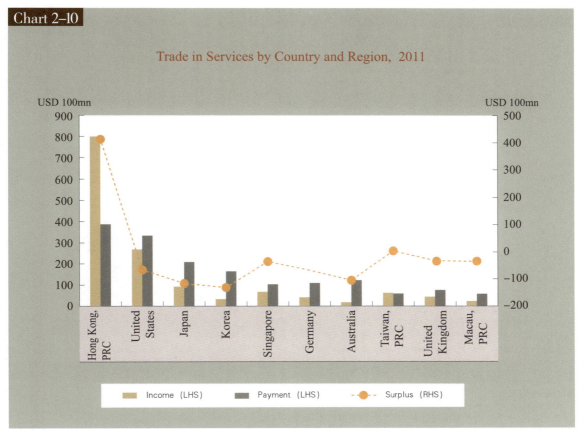

Chart 2–10

Trade in Services by Country and Region, 2011

Sources: SAFE.

(Ⅲ) Direct Investment

Inward foreign direct investment recorded declining inflows and net inflows. In 2011 the inflow of inward foreign direct investment totaled USD 254.3 billion, down 4 percent year on year, and the net inflow was a historical high of USD 220.1 billion but down 10 percent year on year (see Chart 2–11).

Outward direct investment continued to grow with a decreasing net outflow. In 2011 outward direct investment posted a net outflow of USD 67.1 billion, rising by a historical high of USD 1.5 billion. Influenced by the increased clearing of outward direct investment and the withdrawal of loans extended to overseas affiliated enterprises, outward direct investment withdrawals amounted to USD 17.4 billion in 2011, 1.3–fold increase from the withdrawals in 2010, resulting in a net outflow of outward direct investment of USD 49.7 billion, down 14 percent year on year (see Chart 2–12).

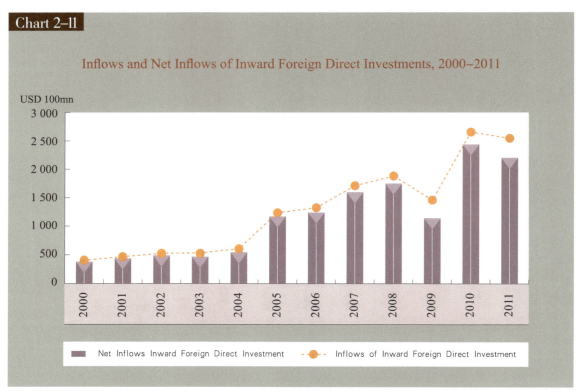

Sources: SAFE.

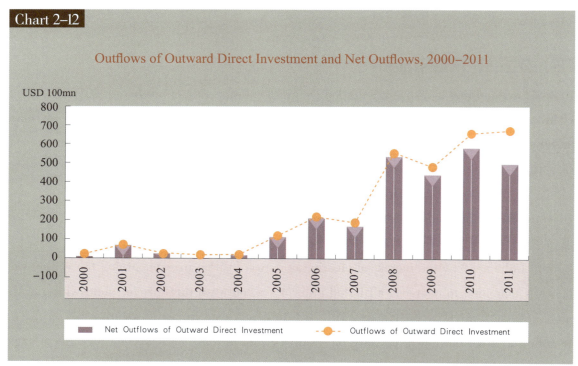

Sources: SAFE.

The net inflows of foreign direct investment were the main sources of China's BOP surplus. In 2011 the surplus in direct investment amounted to USD 170.4 billion, dropping by 8 percent year on year (see Chart 2–13). The contribution of the surplus in foreign direct investment to the total BOP surplus showed a declining trend, and capital flows other than direct investment were having a greater impact on the BOP situation (see Chart 2–13 and Chart 1–6). In 2011 the contribution of the FDI surplus to the BOP surplus was 40 percent, up by 24 percentage points from a low in 2009, indicating that during the financial turmoil direct investment was helping to improve the balance of payments situation and also that international long-term investors continue to be optimistic about China.

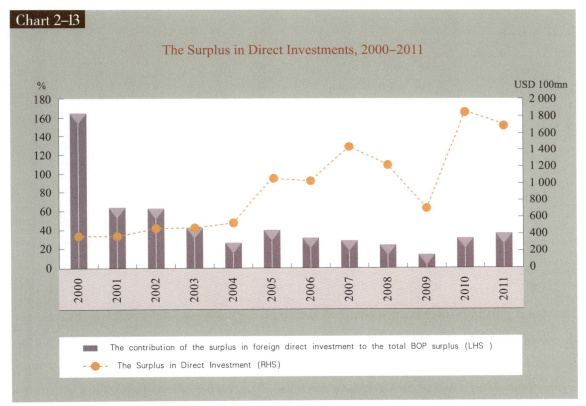

Chart 2–13

The Surplus in Direct Investments, 2000–2011

The contribution of the surplus in foreign direct investment to the total BOP surplus (LHS)

The Surplus in Direct Investment (RHS)

Sources: SAFE.

(Ⅳ) Portfolio Investment

Net inflows of portfolio investment sustained a declining trend. In 2011 net inflows of portfolio investment totaled USD 19.6 billion, down 18 percent year on year. In particular, outward portfolio investment posted a net inflow of USD 6.2 billion, whereas it posted a net outflow of USD 7.6 billion in the first half of the year; inward portfolio investment recorded a net inflow of

USD 13.4 billion, down 58 percent year on year (see Chart 2–14).

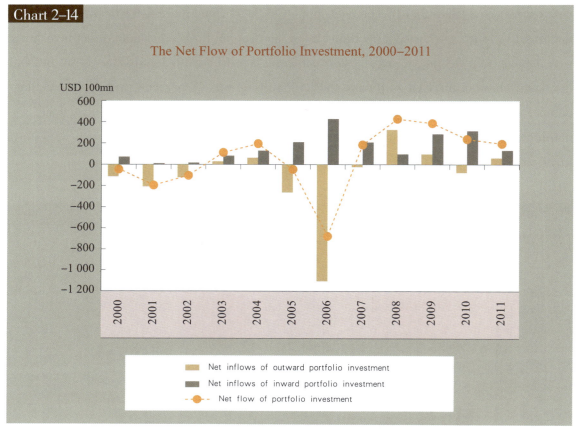

Notes: Positive outward portfolio investment refers to a net inflow and otherwise a net outflow. Positive inward portfolio investment
refers to a net inflow and otherwise a net outflow.
Sources: SAFE.

Outbound portfolio investments declined. In 2011 the sovereign debt crisis in Europe and
the closely related sovereign debt issue in the United States were deteriorating, driving the
fluctuations in international financial markets and leading to increased risk aversion and a
weakening willingness for outward investments. In 2011 outbound equity portfolio investment
outflows and inflows were USD 10.1 billion and USD 11.2 billion respectively, dropping by 49
percent and 2 percent, and net inflows were USD 1.1 billion, posting as a net outflow of USD
8.4 billion in the first half of the year. Outbound debt portfolio investment outflows and inflows
were USD 9.1 billion and USD 14.3 billion respectively, down 37 percent and 7 percent, and
the net inflows were USD 5.1 billion, indicating 6–fold growth year on year. Based on the IIP
statistics, by the end of September 2011 portfolio investment assets accounted for 5.5 percent
of China's foreign assets, which was slightly higher than that in other BRIC countries including

Russia, Brazil, and India, but far lower than that in the developed economies (see Table 2–15). This indicates that outbound portfolio investment by the private sector in the emerging markets, including China, are still limited and insufficient due to policy restrictions and market conditions, which will further impact the pricing power of those countries in international financial markets.

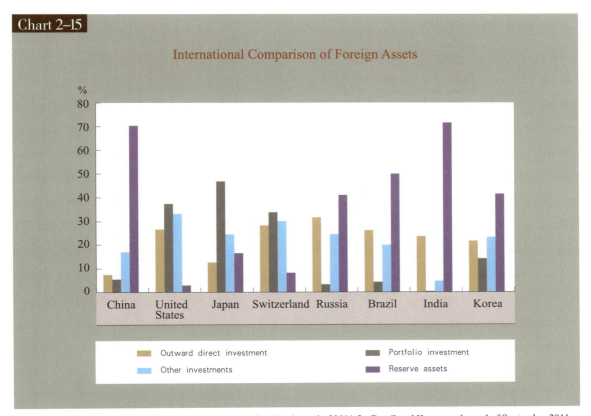

Chart 2–15

International Comparison of Foreign Assets

Notes: The IIP compilation standard adopted. Data are updated to the end of 2011 for Brazil and Korea, to the end of September 2011 for China, Japan, and India, and to the end of 2010 for the United States, Switzerland, and Russia.
Sources: SAFE; CEIC; and the Monetary Authorities of the related Countries.

Inbound portfolio investment decreased. In terms of equity portfolio investment, in 2011 global capital markets experienced a very difficult period because of the shock of the sovereign debt crisis in Europe and the United States. Domestic enterprises faced short position pressures, and the overseas listings and scale of refinancing in the international market dropped from USD 35.4 billion in 2010 to USD 11.6 billion in 2011. QFII investment inflows totaled USD 800 million. Net inflows of inbound equity portfolio investment amounted to USD 5.3 billion, down 83 percent year on year. In terms of debt portfolio investment, net inflows of inbound debt portfolio investment totaled USD 8.1 billion, increasing 24–fold year on year. There are two main reasons for this. One is that beginning from August 2010, three categories of nonresident institutions, such as overseas RMB clearing banks, were authorized to invest in the domestic inter-bank bond market with their RMB position. Another reason is the increased RMB bond issuance in offshore markets, including Hong Kong SAR, by the Ministry of Finance and other domestic institutions.

(V) Trade Credit

Both trade credit[①] assets and liabilities continued to grow (see Chart 2-16). Based on a sample survey of trade credit, by the end of 2011 outstanding trade credit assets amounted to USD 276.9 billion, growing by USD 71 billion and 34 percent year on year. In particular, outstanding export collectables were USD 219.2 billion, increasing by USD 48.2 billion; outstanding advance import payments were USD 57.7 billion, increasing by USD 22.8 billion. Outstanding trade credit liabilities were USD 249.2 billion, up by USD 38 billion and 18 percent year on year. In particular, outstanding import payables were USD 191.4 billion, growing by USD 43.4 billion; outstanding advance export collections were USD 57.8 billion, a decrease of USD 5.3 billion. From the perspective of flows, in 2011 export collectables increased significantly and advance collections decreased, indicating a deterioration in export revenue collection during the crisis period. In terms of the outstanding, that of export collectables increased more than that of advance collections, and import payables increased more than advance payments, indicating that cross-border trade financing focused on liability dollarization based on the real trade background instead of arbitrage by capital inflows.

In the post-crisis period, trade credit is becoming a very important financing channel for domestic enterprises. By the end of 2011, total trade credit assets and liabilities accounted for 15 percent of foreign trade, which was higher than that in 2008 (see Chart 2-17). By maturity, short-term trade credit took a higher position. By the end of 2011, short-term trade credit (less than 1 year) assets of sample enterprises accounted for 90 percent of total trade credit assets, and short-term trade credit liabilities accounted for 93 percent of total trade credit liabilities.

---

① Trade credit refers to payables and collectables of domestic enterprises with nonresidents due to trade transactions. The asset side includes collectables and advance payments, and the liability side includes payables and advance collections. Trade credit reflects an entity's position with its trading partner, excluding trade financing and financing guarantees.

Trade credit assets and liabilities are important components under the item of other investment of the capital and financial account of the BOP. In addition, trade credit liability is a very important source of data on China's external debt statistics. The sum of the outstanding trade credit and the outstanding registered external debt is the total external debt.

In terms of entities, foreign–funded enterprises played a more active role than Chinese–funded enterprises. By the end of 2011, trade credit assets of foreign–funded enterprises accounted for 62 percent of the total trade credit assets of the sample enterprises, and their liabilities accounted for 58 percent of the total trade credit liabilities. Moreover, foreign–funded enterprises tended to arrange capital by collectables and payables, whereas Chinese–funded enterprises tended to arrange capital by advance collections and payments.

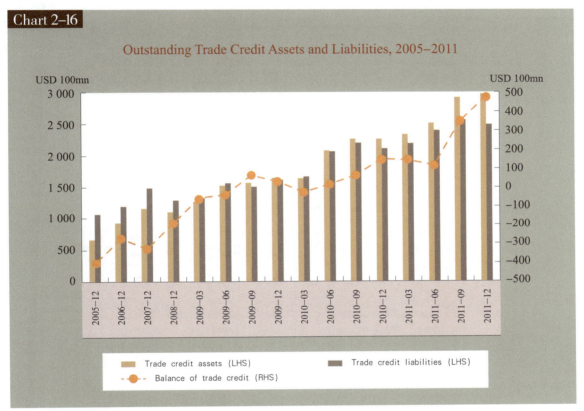

Chart 2–16

Outstanding Trade Credit Assets and Liabilities, 2005–2011

Trade credit assets (LHS)
Trade credit liabilities (LHS)
Balance of trade credit (RHS)

Sources: SAFE.

The trade credit position turned to the position of net assets showed large fluctuations. By the end of 2011, the trade credit position posted net assets of USD 27.7 billion for the first time (in 2010 it posted net liabilities of USD 5.2 billion). This means that capital flows via foreign trade recorded a net outflow. In particular, net assets of trade credit decreased by USD 0.3 billion and USD 2.7 billion during the first and second quarter respectively, but they surged in the third and fourth quarter to USD 23.3 billion and USD 12.7 billion respectively (see Chart 2–16). In the second half of the year, trade credit changed from a net inflow to a net outflow, driven jointly by an accumulation of assets and a drop in liabilities. Due to the sovereign debt crisis and the limited liquidity, domestic enterprises extended more commercial credit to trading partners, leading to growing trade credit assets. Moreover, since the end of September 2011, international financial markets fluctuated sharply, and expectations of a RMB exchange rate appreciation were relieved, leading to accelerated debt payments and decreased trade credit liabilities of domestic enterprises.

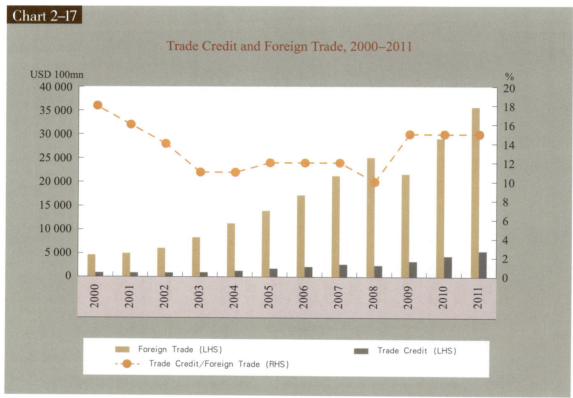

Chart 2–17

Trade Credit and Foreign Trade, 2000–2011

Sources: SAFE.

III. Operations of the Foreign Exchange Market and the RMB Exchange Rate

(I) Reform and Development of the Foreign Exchange Market

Foreign exchange products became more diversified. Foreign exchange options were introduced in both the client market and the inter-bank market. In line with market demand, banks were encouraged to carry out option portfolios for customers to further develop the RMB/foreign exchange derivatives market. In the client market, we also launched RMB/foreign exchange swaps, which optimized the structure of the currency swap market.

New trading currencies were introduced to the foreign exchange market. AUD/RMB and CAD/RMB transactions were launched in the inter-bank foreign exchange market, facilitating bank management of risks and reducing the costs of cross-border trade and currency conversion for investments.

The RMB/foreign exchange market gradually developed a benchmarking system. The inter-bank foreign exchange market successively promulgated the foreign exchange swap curve, the USD implied interest rate curve, the RMB implied volatility curve, and the foreign exchange forward curve, which together formed a relatively comprehensive benchmarking system for the derivatives market. This helped facilitate transactions and manage risks for market participants.

(II) Trends in the RMB Exchange Rate against the Major Foreign Currencies

The RMB continued to appreciate against the USD. At the end of 2011, the RMB mid-price against the USD closed at 6.3009, up 5.1 percent from the end of 2010. Beginning from the exchange rate regime reform in 2005, it has appreciated by 31.4 percent (see Chart 3-1).

The RMB exchange rate showed enhanced two-way fluctuations. In 2011 the spot RMB exchange rate against the USD saw its largest daily floating band (the highest price minus the lowest price) at 96 bps (in 2010 it was 70 bps). The largest daily fluctuation of the trading price over the mid-price peaked at 0.18 percent (in 2010 it was 0.10 percent). In the 244 trading days, there were 71 appreciations and 58 depreciations against the mid-price, as well as 115 days of two-way around the mid-price. The three directions showed a more balanced distribution (see Chart 3-1).

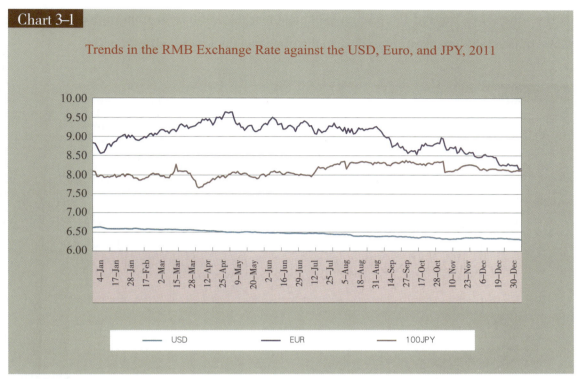

Chart 3–1

Trends in the RMB Exchange Rate against the USD, Euro, and JPY, 2011

Sources: CFETS.

Table 3–1　Fluctuations of the Spot RMB Exchange Rate against the USD in the Inter–Bank Foreign Exchange Market, 2006–2011

Year	The Largest Fluctuation of the Trading Price over the Mid-Price (Daily Average)	Double Direction Fluctuation around the Mid-Price	Appreciation over the Mid-Price	Depreciation over the Mid-Price
		(Percentage in terms of trading days)		
2006	0.07%	83.1%	13.6%	3.3%
2007	0.11%	66.5%	25.6%	7.9%
2008	0.15%	65.4%	16.3%	18.3%
2009	0.04%	70.5%	12.3%	17.2%
2010	0.10%	61.6%	23.1%	15.3%
2011	0.18%	47.1%	29.1%	23.8%

Since late September, with the changes in the relationship of domestic foreign exchange supply and demand, the inter–bank market saw fluctuations of the trading price over the mid–price, hitting the upper limit of the 0.5% floating band for several days, which meant that the RMB hit the lower limit against the USD (see Chart 3–2). But when the trading price at the lower limit was not equal to the devaluation of the RMB exchange rate in the fourth quarter, the RMB mid–price appreciated by 0.9 percent against the USD. Meanwhile, the Central Bank sold foreign exchange reserves at the lower–limit to provide foreign exchange liquidity to the market; the lower limit of the foreign exchange market is different from the equity market where transactions are totally closed when the price hits the lower limit.

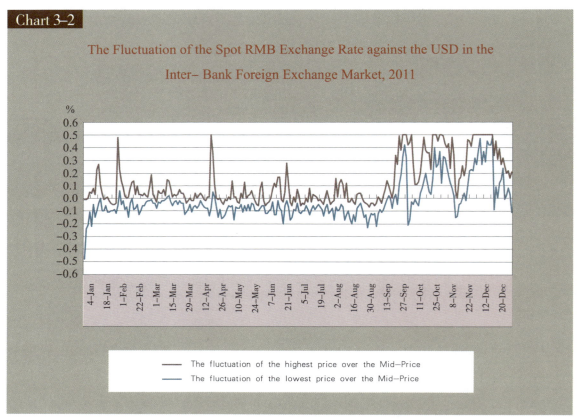

Chart 3–2

The Fluctuation of the Spot RMB Exchange Rate against the USD in the Inter– Bank Foreign Exchange Market, 2011

——— The fluctuation of the highest price over the Mid–Price
——— The fluctuation of the lowest price over the Mid–Price

Sources: CFETS.

The unilateral expectations of the RMB exchange rate were expected to change. From the beginning of 2011 to the middle of September of 2011, both the domestic and overseas markets maintained appreciation expectations of the RMB exchange rate against the USD. However, due to the weak recovery of the global economy, the continuous acceleration of the European debt crisis, the slowing down of the Chinese economy, and a series of other domestic and overseas factors, pressures for a RMB appreciation were reduced, changing from appreciation to depreciation pressures in late September in the domestic market and in early December in the overseas market. In 2011 by observing the 1–year forward price, the implied RMB appreciation expectation peaked at 1.9 percent in the domestic market and 3.0 percent in the overseas market, and the RMB depreciation expectation peaked at 0.6 percent in the domestic market and 1.8 percent in the overseas market（see Chart 3–3 and Column 3）.

Chart 3–3

The 1–Year RMB Appreciation Expectation against the USD in the Domestic and Overseas Markets, 2011

Sources: CFETS, Reuters.

Box 3

The Price Determination Mechanism in the Hong Kong Offshore RMB Market

The Hong Kong offshore RMB market began in 2004 when individuals could exchange RMB with Hong Kong banks and it developed in 2009 when a pilot program in which RMB settlements for cross–border trade was launched. As an international financial center, Hong Kong made good use of its own advantages and closely followed the process of gradual opening of the mainland financial market. As a result there was a steady growth in entities, products, and the size of the Hong Kong RMB market. Until now, the market has formulated two exchange rates for spot and forward transactions, and has shaped three curves for the spot exchange rate (CNH Spot), the deliverable forward rate (CNH DF), and the non–deliverable forward rate (CNY NDF).

Theoreticaly, the prices of one product in different markets should converge if there are no special arbitrage restrictions. Though the RMB is not fully convertible, as more channels became available for cross–border RMB flows, the arbitraging mechanism between the domestic and offshore markets drove the the prices in the two markets to converge, thereby avoiding a large deviation between the two prices.

Due to the different sizes of the domestic and offshore markets and the managed floating RMB exchange rate regime, a feature of the price determination mechanism of the offshore market is that its baseline is the price in the domestic market. Its own market supply and demand also impact price movements. Overseas investors were the main RMB users and domestic businesses were the main RMB suppliers. Both sides forced offshore prices to fluctuate in different directions around the domestic price (see Chart C3–1).

Chart C3–1

Factors of the Market Supply and Demand That Impact the Offshore Price

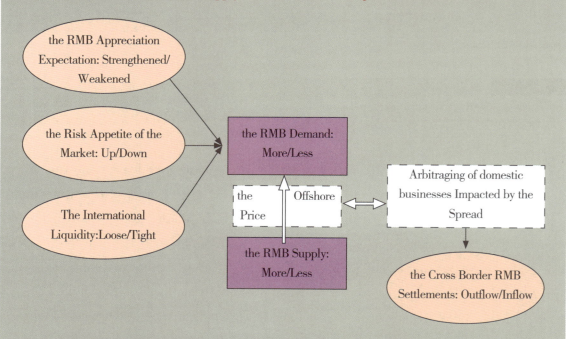

In late September 2011, the spot RMB exchange rate in the Hong Kong market (CNH) changed from a premium to a discount against the domestic market. At the largest spread, the price of one dollar in the offshore market was 0.12 yuan (1 200 bps) more than that in the domestic market. Thereafter, the spread began to narrow. Until the end of

2011, the small discount continued. As the European debt crisis evolved and the views of shorting China emerged, offshore investors changed their risk appetite, liquidity, and exchange rate expectations. As a result, the offshore price deviated from the domestic price and domestic businesses began to arbitrage, bringing the two prices to once again converge (see Chart C3–2).

Chart C3–2

Trends in the RMB Exchange Rate against the USD in the Offshore and Domestic Markets, 2010 to 2011

Notes: CNH and CNY represent the prices in the offshore and domestic markets respectively, both of which are the spot closing prices.
Sources: CFETS, Reuters.

The relationship between the offshore and domestic prices is characterized by the following three features:

First, the offshore price may overreact. As the market would typically read the rapid change in the domestic price as an indication of appreciation, the expectation might drive the offshore RMB price to change more rapidly than the domestic price. In particular, since the offshore market is highly open, the features of the offshore RMB may become more similar to that of some Asian currencies, such as the SGD and THB, which are not only impacted by the domestic market, but also part of the global foreign exchange market. In the short term, the offshore price could deviate from the domestic price and especially from the domestic mid-price which serves as the benchmark, revealing large volatility.

Second, the offshore and domestic markets developed by different steps, exerting an influence on the spread of the prices in the two markets. With respect to market participants, more investment banks, hedge funds, and banks outside Hong Kong joined the offshore market, which changed the size and structure of RMB users. Different from the initial period when transactions were confined within trades, non-trade transactions increased and dominated the market. More importantly, those changes complicated the factors that impacted the demand for RMB. As a result, the purchase or sale of RMB did not necessarily indicate a change in RMB appreciation expectations. With respect to products, the RMB exchange rate and interest rate products gradually diversified. This not only changed the pricing mechanism in the offshore market, but also attracted more participants to the market, influencing RMB supply and demand.

Third, there was a two-track policy in the offshore RMB market. According to current policies, the People's Bank of China uses clearing banks to provide the participating banks channels for RMB conversion. The People's Bank of China also applies a double direction quota control to the clearing banks when they purchase and sell RMB in the domestic inter-bank foreign exchange market. The participating banks can only balance their RMB positions for trade-related transactions through the clearing banks, while non-trade transactions have to be balanced through the offshore market. Therefore, the RMB price for trade-related transactions is different from that for non-trade transactions in the offshore market, with the former based on the domestic price as a benchmark and the latter more dependent on market supply and demand.

The RMB effective exchange rate further appreciated. According to the BIS data, in 2011 the nominal effective exchange rate of the RMB appreciated by 4.9 percent against the basket of currencies. Deducting inflation, the real effective exchange rate of the RMB appreciated by 6.1 percent. Since the RMB exchange rate regime reform in 2005, the nominal and real effective exchange rates of the RMB appreciated by 21.2 percent and 30.3 percent respectively（see Chart 3-4）. Among the 61 economies observed by the BIS, in 2011 the RMB ranked third in terms of the extent of the appreciation of the nominal effective exchange rate and ranked second in terms of the extent of the appreciation of the real effective exchange rate. In other BRIC countries, including Russia, Brazil, India, and South Africa, on average the nominal effective exchange rate depreciated by 10.0 percent and the real effective exchange rate depreciated by 7.4 percent. By comparison, the RMB showed a steady performance among the currencies of the emerging markets (see Box 4).

Chart 3-4

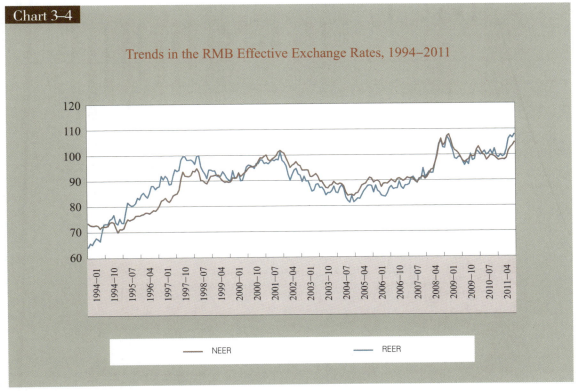

Trends in the RMB Effective Exchange Rates, 1994–2011

NEER   REER

Sources: BIS.

Box 4

The Reasons for the Development of the Exchange Rates of the Emerging Markets in 2011

In 2011 the external environment and the domestic economic and credit cycles worked together to impact the currencies of the emerging markets, which appreciated at the beginning of the year and depreciated thereafter, showing large volatility. Actually, the currencies of the major emerging markets all depreciated against the USD. According to the BIS, the multilateral exchange rates of the emerging markets also depreciated with volatility (see Chart C4–1).

Chart C4–1

Trends in the Exchange Rates of the Major Emerging Markets

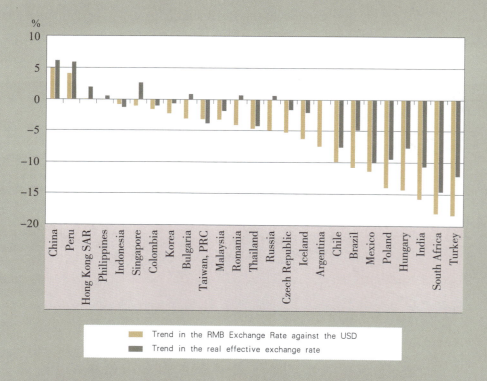

Sources: BIS, Bloomberg.

The cross–border capital flows contributed greatly to the large volatility of the exchange rates of the emerging markets. In the first half of 2011, investors cared more about the economic growth of the U.S. and Europe than about the European debt crisis. The credit environment during that period was relatively loose and the emerging markets experienced net capital inflows. At the end of July, the EMCI went up by 3.3 percent from the end of the previous year. After the repeated shocks from the U.S. debt ceiling and the European debt crisis in August, the banking sector in the U.S. and Europe faced strong pressures to deleverage, resulting in a tight credit environment and net capital outflows from the emerging markets. After the appreciation at the beginning of the year, most of the currencies of the emerging markets depreciated, with the EMCI at the end of December down 13 percent from the end of July and down 9.1 percent from the end of the previous year.

The different conditions in the trade balances of the emerging markets drove their currency divergencies, while countries with a trade deficit were more significantly impacted by external factors, including changes in the risk appetite of investors and the direction of capital flows. If the capital inflows did not effectively help the countries with trade deficits develop their trade competitiveness and improve their solvency, the debt capital would eventually withdraw. As for the BRIC countries in 2011, the real effective exchange rates of India and South Africa depreciated by more than 10 percent because investors worried that the trade deficit was unsustainable and would eventually hurt economic growth.

According to forecasts, the exchange rates of the emerging markets will continue to fluctuate with large volatility, following the changes in risk appetites in global financial markets. Though the emerging markets may support their exchange rates due to the high potential of economic growth, their financial markets have quite limited depth and width. According to the BIS, by the end of June 2011 the total stock of the domestic bond markets of the 26 major emerging markets together accounted for only 13.4 percent of the global bond market and 80.7 percent of the US Treasury market. From an economic perspective, the emerging markets did not decouple from the advanced economies and those depending on exports were quite vulnerable to changes in external demand.

(III) Transactions in the Foreign Exchange Market

In 2011, the cumulative trading volume of the RMB /foreign exchange market totaled USD 8.64 trillion, with an average daily trading volume of USD 35.4 billion. The total trading volume went up by 26.9 percent from the previous year, of which the client market saw USD 3.10 trillion and the inter–bank market saw USD 5.54 trillion [1] (see Table 3–2).

Foreign exchange spot transactions grew steadily. In 2011 foreign exchange spot transactions in the client market accumulated to USD 2.7 trillion (implementation of forwards is not included), up 25 percent from the previous year. Cumulative foreign exchange spot transactions in the inter–bank market totaled USD 3.55 trillion, with an daily average trading volume of USD 14.6 billion, which was up 16 percent from 2010. In 2011 spot transactions accounted for 72 percent of the total transactions in the market, the lowest in history (see Chart 3–5). This shows that the product structures in the domestic market were more diversified and derivatives were more broadly accepted by market participants.

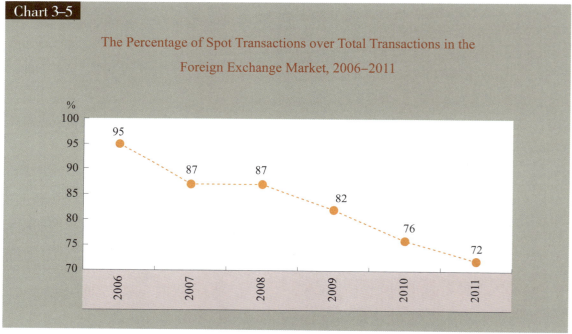

Chart 3–5

The Percentage of Spot Transactions over Total Transactions in the Foreign Exchange Market, 2006–2011

Sources: SAFE , CFETS.

Foreign exchange forward transactions rose rapidly. In 2011 cumulative foreign exchange forward transactions in the client market reached USD 387.1 billion, up 37 percent from 2010. In the client market, purchases of foreign exchange reached USD 191.3 billion and sales reached USD

---

[1] In the client market, the trading volume was calculated as the total purchases and sales of foreign exchange by clients, the inter bank market only took the data for one side. The same below.

195.8 billion, increasing by 16 percent and 67 percent respectively from 2010. Cumulative foreign exchange forward transactions in the inter−bank market totaled USD 214.6 billion, with an average daily trading volume of USD 880 million, which was 5.5 times from that in 2010.

Foreign exchange and currency swap transactions increased greatly. In 2011 cumulative foreign exchange and currency swap transactions in the client market reached USD 14.2 billion, 1.2 times that in the 2010. Cumulative foreign exchange and currency swap transactions in the inter−bank market reached USD 1.77 trillion, up 37 percent from 2010. The average daily trading volume stood at USD 7.26 billion.

Foreign exchange options developed from zero. On April 1, 2011, foreign exchange options were formally launched in both the client market and the inter−bank market. In terms of the nominal principal of foreign exchange options, the inter−bank market saw a total trading volume of USD 1.01 billion in 2011. A major part of these transactions were short−term USD options of less than 3 months and most were foreign exchange put options. The client market saw a total trading volume of USD 0.87 billion, focusing on foreign exchange call options. At the end of December, the implied volatility of the 3−month and 1−year RMB/USD options in the inter−bank market stood at 3.23 percent and 4.54 percent respectively, higher by 0.1 and 0.2 percentage point of that of the non−delivered options overseas (NDO) during the same period.

Table 3−2　Transactions in the RMB/ Foreign Exchange Market, 2011

Products	Trading Volume (USD 100 mm)
Spot	**62 544**
Client Market	27 005
Inter-Bank Foreign Exchange Market	35 538
Forward	**6 017**
Client Market	3 871
Inter-Bank Foreign Exchange Market	2 146
Less than 3 months (including 3 months)	1 282
3 months to 1 year (including 1 year)	815
More than 1 year	49

(continued)

Products	Trading Volume (USD 100 mm)
Foreign Exchange and Currency Swaps	**17 853**
Client Market	142
Inter-Bank Foreign Exchange Market	17 710
Less than 3 months (including 3 months)	16 433
3 months to 1 year (including 1 year)	1 244
More than 1 year	34
Option	**19**
Client Market	8.7
Foreign Exchange Call Option /RMB Put Option	8.1
Foreign Exchange Put Option /RMB Call Option	0.6
Inter-Bank Foreign Exchange Market	10.1
Foreign Exchange Call Option /RMB Put Option	2.4
Foreign Exchange Put Option /RMB Call Option	7.7
Less than 3 months (including 3 months)	9.4
3 months to 1 year (including 1 year)	0.7
More than 1 year	0
Total	**86 431**
Client Market	31 027
Inter-Bank Foreign Exchange Market	55 405
Spot	62 544
Forward	6 017
Foreign Exchange and Currency Swaps	17 853
Option	19

Note: The trading volumes here are unilateral transactions and data use round numbers.
Sources: SAFE, CFETS.

The currency pairs increased rapidly. In 2011 the nine currency pairs saw a total trading volume of USD 94.7 billion (see Table 3–3). The spot transactions, which contributed the most to the total transactions, saw a total trading volume of USD 85.7 billion, with an average daily trading volume of USD 350 million and an increase by 69 percent from 2010. Ever since the currency pairs were launched in the inter-bank foreign exchange market in 2005, the USD/

HKD and the EURO/USD pairs have dominated the market, along with the largely shrinking USD/JPY and the rapidly growing AUD/USD (see Chart 3–6). This trend was in line with the development of the international foreign exchange market and reflected economic relations between Mainland China and Hong Kong.

Table 3–3　Currency Pairs in the Inter–Bank Foreign Exchange Spot Market, 2011

Currency Pairs	EURO/USD	AUD/USD	GBP/USD	USD/JPY	USD/CAD	USD/CHF	USD/HKD	EURO/JPY	USD/SGD
Volume ($ 100 million)	321.3	86.4	25.6	23.0	2.5	9.9	381.4	1.3	5.3
Proportion (%)	37.5	10.1	3.0	2.7	0.3	1.2	44.5	0.2	0.6
YoY Growth (%)	160.7	256.6	–6.5	–31.5	–37.7	246.6	35.6	73.6	8.4
The Number of Deals	22 196	6 190	1 377	2 708	637	506	5 624	71	606

Sources: CFETS.

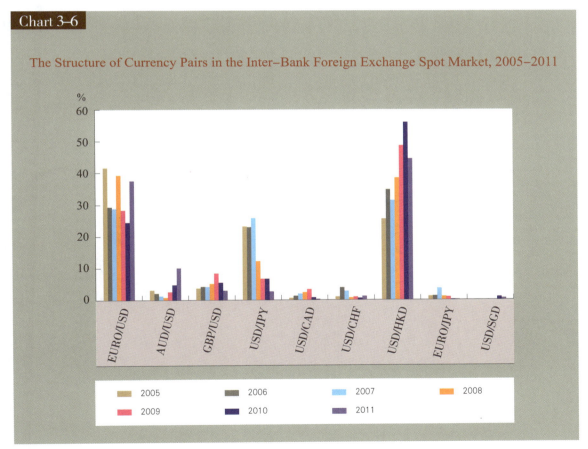

Chart 3–6

The Structure of Currency Pairs in the Inter–Bank Foreign Exchange Spot Market, 2005–2011

Sources: CFETS.

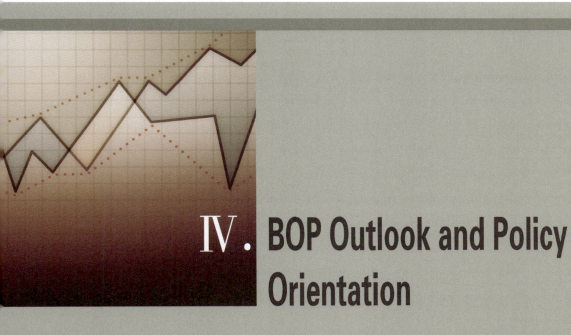

IV. BOP Outlook and Policy Orientation

(I) Outlook

In 2012 the global economic recovery will slow down and uncertainties in international capital flows will remain. With surging government debt, the developed economies, including those in Europe and the United States, will continue implementing tight fiscal policies, leaving less room for economic improvements. According to the latest March 2012 forecast of the IMF, the global economy is projected to expand by 3.3 percent, 0.5 percentage point lower than the growth rate in 2011. Total global trade volume is projected to expand by 3.8 percent, 3.1 percentage points lower than the rate in 2011. Meanwhile, loose monetary policies in the major developed economies, including those in the United States and Europe, will continue, contributing to adequacy in global liquidity. As international financial supervision further tightens, the European sovereign debt crisis may spread to other highly indebted Euro zone countries. With interactions between banking sector risks and sovereign default risks, and with unstable factors including uncertainties in geo-political events, risk aversion in global capital may intensify, leading to more volatile cross-border capital flows.

In 2012 China's economy will expand stably, with stronger endogenous economic growth. Although it has set a lower annual GDP growth rate target for 2012, China still has a promising economic growth perspective fueled by long-term development factors such as industrialization and urbanization. According to the latest forecast of the IMF, China's GDP growth rate is expected to reach 8.2 percent, among the highest growth rates worldwide. The quality and efficiency of economic development will be further improved. By accelerating the transformation of its economic development pattern and adjusting its economic structure, China will witness a much stronger effect of domestic demand on economic growth and a falling CPI. Meanwhile, expanding consumption demand, increasing imports, and implementing the "going abroad" policies will be more firmly put into effect.

In sum, China's balance of payments will maintain a surplus, but the volume of the overall surplus will decrease sharply in 2012. In the short run, as the structural problems of the developed countries remain unsolved, and the international economic and financial situations continue to be unsteady, China may encounter more volatile cross-border capital flows. Meanwhile, with more balanced supply and demand of foreign exchange, and diversified market expectations for the RMB exchange rate, in 2012 China will witness a trend of two-way fluctuations in the RMB exchange rate, with both appreciations and deprecations.

Box 5

Development, Evolution, and Outlook for the Sovereign Debt Crisis

Since 2010, the European soverign debt crisis that began in Greece has rapidly spread to less-developed Euro zone countries. The debt problems of Japan and the United States have also evoked great concern. The development and evolution of the sovereign debt crisis was mainly affected by the following factors:

First, the sovereign debt level. Looking at the total government debt relative to GDP across the major economies, Japan recorded a ratio of 208.2 percent, Greece 165.4 percent, Italy 120.1 percent, and the United States 99.5 percent. Compared with the ratios at the end of 2010, the major countries experienced a rising ratio, with Japan being the only exception. Japan, even with the highest debt level, recorded a decreasing ratio. The persistent high government debt level increases contagion risks, rapidly increasing the possibility of a sovereign credit downgrading. In August 2011, Standard & Poor's downgraded the United States' sovereign credit rating from AAA to AA+. Since 2009 Greece's sovereign credit rating has been downgraded 11 times from A- to its current CC.

Second, progress in the crisis bailout. The International Monetary Fund, the European Union, and the European Central Bank have implemented a series of bailout measures in an attempt to stop the deterioration and to control the risk of contagion of the European sovereign crisis. These measures include: establishing the permanent European Stability Mechanism (ESM) and expanding the bailout capacity of the mechanism; providing insurance to the banking sector debt and injecting captial; providing capital for the bailout to the crisis-stricken countries, including Greece, and arranging Private Sector Involvement (PSI) with Greek private investors. By the end of 2011, the confirmed total bailout capacity reached Euro 273 billion, with Euro 110 billion for Greece, Euro 85 billion for Ireland, and Euro 78 billion for Portugal. The bailout capital has been provided in batches according to the progress in fiscal tighening in the rescued countries.

Third, development of global deleveraging. Deleveraging is a self-rescue measure for households, entities, and banks during periods of crisis. Take the banking sector for example, to control total credit or to sell assets to cut down the level of liability is a major way to deleverage. By deleveraging, banks can restore and restructure their balance sheets, but this will affect borrowings and consumption by households and entities.

Fourth, the quantitative easing monetary policies of the central banks. During the crisis, to stimulate an economic recovery, the Federal Reserve of the United States promised to maintain the targeted zero interest rate at least until 2014. It also implemented "twist operations" by selling short-term treasury bills and buying back long-term treasury bonds. The European Central Bank also maintained the benchmark rate at 1 percent, and loosened monetary policy by decreasing interest rates, buying back bonds, and increasing the supply of liquidity. By the end of February 2012, the European Central Bank had bought back Euro 219 billion of treasury bonds and had injected about Euro 617 billion into the banking sector by means of MRO and LTRO. The Bank of England's holdings of government bonds have reached around Sterling 241 billion since the bank implemented its quantitative easing monetary policy. The Bank of Japan also maintained the targeted overnight interest rate at 0.1 percent, a very low level.

At the international level, international organizations and global financial cooperation platforms including the G20 and the International Monetary Fund worked with the crisis-stricken countries to actively discuss and seek solutions. Fundamentally, the steady recovery of the global economy and the subsequent economic growth to digest the debt is the ultimate solution to the crisis. Prior to that, uncertainties in global economic and financial markets will persist, the sovereign debt crisis in the major developed countries may continue, and the emerging market economies may encounter new shocks. The evolution in the patterns of global capital flows will still require close attention.

(II) Policy Orientation

In 2012 China will continue transforming its economic development pattern, promoting strategic economic structural adjustments, and expanding domestic demand, especially demand for consumption. Meanwhile, it will transform its economic growth to a pattern of more harmonized consumption, investments, and net exports. The country also aims to achieve more balanced foreign trade by simultaneously stabilizing exports and promoting imports. Through measures such as improving the quality of FDI, actively implementing the "going-global" strategy, and allowing resident investors to invest abroad, the country will further improve its balance of payments situation.

Based on the "seeking improvement through steady progress" macro–management plan, the authorities will solidify and reinforce their achievements in fighting against the shocks of international financial crises and will enhance their administrative capacity to service the real economy. The major work will include:

First, firmly sticking to a risk bottom line. Structuring a mechanism to avoid shocks of cross–border capital inflows. Closely monitoring both abnormal cross–border inflows and outflows, and reinforcing the package of policy instruments.

Second, focusing on trade and investment facilitation, promoting foreign exchange administrative reform for foreign trade, steadily promoting capital account liberalization, and expanding the channels for external investments.

Third, improving transaction mechanisms, enriching risk–hedging products, and vigorously developing the foreign exchange market.

Fourth, improving the system and mechanism for foreign exchange reserve management, and achieving the goals of safety, liquidity, and value appreciation in reserve assets management.

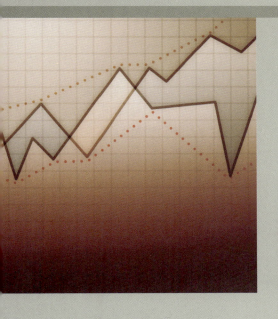

附　　录　统计资料
Appendix　Statistics

一、国际收支①

I. Balance of Payments

中国国际收支交易规模及其占GDP比例 ● China's Scale of BOP Transactions and Its Ratio to GDP

国际收支交易规模（左轴）Scale of BOP Transactions (LHS)

占GDP比例（右轴）Ratio of Scale of BOP Transactions to GDP (RHS)

亿美元
USD 100 million

①资料来源：国家外汇管理局；IMF《国际收支统计》、《国际金融统计》；CEIC Asia Database。
Sources：State Administration of Foreign Exchange；IMF，*Balance of Payments Statistics*，*International Financial Statistics*；CEIC Asia Database.

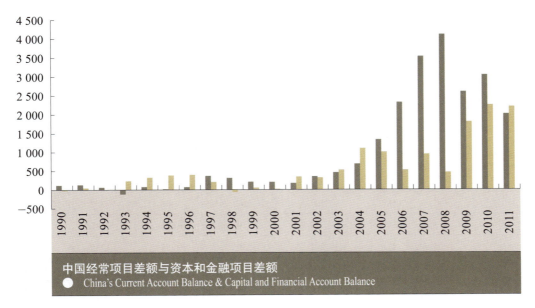

中国经常项目差额与资本和金融项目差额
● China's Current Account Balance & Capital and Financial Account Balance

■ 经常项目差额 Current Account Balance

■ 资本和金融项目差额 Capital and Financial Account Balance

亿 美 元
USD 100 million

中国国际收支概览表（1）

China's Balance of Payments Abridged (1)

项目 Item ╲ 年份 Year	1982	1983	1984	1985	1986	1987
一、经常项目差额 Current Account Balance	**57**	**42**	**20**	**−114**	**−70**	**3**
贷方 Credit	254	254	293	301	312	405
借方 Debit	197	211	273	415	382	402
A.货物和服务差额 Goods and Services Balance	**48**	**26**	**1**	**−125**	**−74**	**3**
贷方 Credit	237	233	268	283	298	392
借方 Debit	189	207	267	408	372	389
a.货物差额 Goods Balance	**42**	**20**	**0**	**−131**	**−91**	**−17**
贷方 Credit	211	207	239	251	258	347
借方 Debit	169	187	239	382	349	364
b.服务差额 Services Balance	**6**	**6**	**0**	**6**	**18**	**20**
贷方 Credit	26	26	29	31	40	44
借方 Debit	20	20	29	25	23	25
B.收益差额 Income Balance	**4**	**12**	**15**	**8**	**0**	**−2**
贷方 Credit	10	15	19	14	9	10
借方 Debit	6	3	4	5	9	12
C.经常转移差额 Current Transfers Balance	**5**	**5**	**4**	**2**	**4**	**2**
贷方 Credit	7	6	6	4	5	4
借方 Debit	2	1	2	2	1	2
二、资本和金融项目差额 Capital and Financial Account Balance	**−17**	**−14**	**−38**	**85**	**65**	**27**
贷方 Credit	36	30	45	212	213	192
借方 Debit	53	44	83	127	148	164
A.资本账户差额 Capital Account Balance	—	—	—	—	—	—
贷方 Credit	—	—	—	—	—	—
借方 Debit	—	—	—	—	—	—
B.金融账户差额 Financial Account Balance	**−17**	**−14**	**−38**	**85**	**65**	**27**
贷方 Credit	36	30	45	212	213	192
借方 Debit	53	44	83	127	148	164

单位：亿美元
Unit: USD 100 million

项目 Item / 年份 Year	1982	1983	1984	1985	1986	1987
1. 直接投资差额 Direct Investment Balance	4	8	13	13	18	17
贷方 Credit	4	9	14	20	22	23
借方 Debit	0	1	1	6	5	6
2. 证券投资差额 Portfolio Investment Balance	0	−6	−16	30	16	11
贷方 Credit	0	2	9	30	16	12
借方 Debit	0	8	26	0	0	1
3. 其他投资差额 Other Investment Balance	−21	−16	−34	41	32	0
贷方 Credit	31	20	22	162	175	157
借方 Debit	52	35	56	120	143	157
三、储备资产变动额 Reserve Assets	−42	−27	5	54	17	−17
贷方 Credit	1	—	7	56	19	—
借方 Debit	43	27	2	2	1	17
其中：外汇储备差额 Foreign Exchange Reserves	−43	−19	7	56	12	−15
四、净误差与遗漏 Net Errors and Omissions	3	−2	12	−25	−12	−14

中国国际收支概览表（2）

China's Balance of Payments Abridged（2）

项目 Item	年份 Year 1988	1989	1990	1991	1992	1993
一、经常项目差额 Current Account Balance	−38	−43	120	133	64	−119
贷方 Credit	479	502	608	705	856	922
借方 Debit	518	545	488	572	792	1 041
A.货物和服务差额 Goods and Services Balance	−41	−49	107	116	50	−118
贷方 Credit	459	478	574	659	788	866
借方 Debit	500	528	467	543	738	983
a.货物差额 Goods Balance	−53	−56	92	87	52	−107
贷方 Credit	411	432	515	589	696	757
借方 Debit	464	488	424	502	644	863
b.服务差额 Services Balance	13	7	15	29	−2	−11
贷方 Credit	49	46	59	70	92	109
借方 Debit	36	39	44	41	94	120
B.收益差额 Income Balance	−2	2	11	8	2	−13
贷方 Credit	15	19	30	37	56	44
借方 Debit	16	17	20	29	53	57
C.经常转移差额 Current Transfers Balance	4	4	3	8	12	12
贷方 Credit	6	5	4	9	12	13
借方 Debit	1	1	1	1	1	1
二、资本和金融项目差额 Capital and Financial Account Balance	53	64	−28	46	−3	235
贷方 Credit	203	212	204	203	302	508
借方 Debit	150	148	232	157	305	274
A.资本账户差额 Capital Account Balance	—	—	—	—	—	—
贷方 Credit	—	—	—	—	—	—
借方 Debit	—	—	—	—	—	—
B.金融账户差额 Financial Account Balance	53	64	−28	46	−3	235
贷方 Credit	203	212	204	203	302	508
借方 Debit	150	148	232	157	305	274

单位：亿美元
Unit: USD 100 million

项目 Item / 年份 Year	1988	1989	1990	1991	1992	1993
1.直接投资差额 Direct Investment Balance	**23**	**26**	**27**	**35**	**72**	**231**
贷方 Credit	32	34	35	44	112	275
借方 Debit	9	8	8	9	40	44
2.证券投资差额 Portfolio Investment Balance	**9**	**−2**	**−2**	**2**	**−1**	**31**
贷方 Credit	12	1	—	6	9	50
借方 Debit	3	3	2	3	9	20
3.其他投资差额 Other Investment Balance	**20**	**40**	**−52**	**9**	**−74**	**−27**
贷方 Credit	159	177	169	154	182	183
借方 Debit	138	137	221	145	256	210
三、储备资产变动额 Reserve Assets	**−5**	**−22**	**−61**	**−111**	**21**	**−18**
贷方 Credit	1	1	—	—	24	1
借方 Debit	5	23	61	111	3	18
其中：外汇储备差额 Foreign Exchange Reserves	−4	−22	−55	−106	23	−18
四、净误差与遗漏 Net Errors and Omissions	**−10**	**1**	**−31**	**−68**	**−83**	**−98**

中国国际收支概览表（3）

China's Balance of Payments Abridged (3)

项目 Item / 年份 Year	1994	1995	1996	1997	1998	1999
一、经常项目差额 Current Account Balance	**77**	**16**	**72**	**370**	**315**	**211**
贷方 Credit	1 264	1 543	1 814	2 184	2 177	2 347
借方 Debit	1 188	1 526	1 741	1 815	1 862	2 135
A.货物和服务差额 Goods and Services Balance	**74**	**120**	**176**	**428**	**438**	**306**
贷方 Credit	1 189	1 472	1 717	2 072	2 074	2 210
借方 Debit	1 116	1 353	1 541	1 644	1 636	1 903
a.货物差额 Goods Balance	**73**	**181**	**195**	**462**	**466**	**360**
贷方 Credit	1 026	1 281	1 511	1 827	1 835	1 947
借方 Debit	953	1 101	1 315	1 364	1 369	1 587
b.服务差额 Services Balance	**1**	**−61**	**−20**	**−34**	**−28**	**−53**
贷方 Credit	164	191	206	246	239	262
借方 Debit	163	252	226	280	267	316
B.收益差额 Income Balance	**−10**	**−118**	**−124**	**−110**	**−166**	**−145**
贷方 Credit	57	52	73	57	56	83
借方 Debit	68	170	198	167	222	228
C.经常转移差额 Current Transfers Balance	**13**	**14**	**21**	**51**	**43**	**49**
贷方 Credit	18	18	24	55	47	54
借方 Debit	4	4	2	3	4	4
二、资本和金融项目差额 Capital and Financial Account Balance	**326**	**387**	**400**	**210**	**−63**	**52**
贷方 Credit	618	677	710	926	893	918
借方 Debit	291	290	310	716	956	866
A.资本账户差额 Capital Account Balance	**—**	**—**	**—**	**−0**	**−0**	**−0**
贷方 Credit	—	—	—	—	—	—
借方 Debit	—	—	—	0	0	0
B.金融账户差额 Financial Account Balance	**326**	**387**	**400**	**210**	**−63**	**52**
贷方 Credit	618	677	710	926	893	918
借方 Debit	291	290	310	716	956	865

单位：亿美元
Unit: USD 100 million

项目 Item	年份 Year	1994	1995	1996	1997	1998	1999
1.直接投资差额 Direct Investment Balance		**318**	**338**	**381**	**417**	**411**	**370**
贷方 Credit		338	377	424	454	456	410
借方 Debit		20	39	43	38	45	40
2.证券投资差额 Portfolio Investment Balance		**35**	**8**	**17**	**69**	**−37**	**−112**
贷方 Credit		45	18	34	92	19	18
借方 Debit		10	10	16	23	56	130
3.其他投资差额 Other Investment Balance		**−27**	**40**	**2**	**−276**	**−437**	**−205**
贷方 Credit		235	282	253	380	418	489
借方 Debit		262	241	251	655	854	695
三、储备资产变动额 Reserve Assets		**−305**	**−225**	**−317**	**−357**	**−64**	**−85**
贷方 Credit		—	—	—	0	—	13
借方 Debit		305	225	317	357	64	98
其中：外汇储备差额 Foreign Exchange Reserves		−304	−220	−315	−349	−51	−97
四、净误差与遗漏 Net Errors and Omissions		**−98**	**−178**	**−155**	**−223**	**−187**	**−178**

中国国际收支概览表（4）

China's Balance of Payments Abridged (4)

项目 Item ＼ 年份 Year	2000	2001	2002	2003	2004	2005
一、经常项目差额 Current Account Balance	**205**	**174**	**354**	**459**	**687**	**1 341**
贷方 Credit	2 990	3 179	3 875	5 196	7 007	9 036
借方 Debit	2 785	3 005	3 521	4 737	6 320	7 695
A. 货物和服务差额 Goods and Services Balance	**289**	**281**	**374**	**361**	**493**	**1 248**
贷方 Credit	2 796	2 994	3 654	4 850	6 558	8 369
借方 Debit	2 507	2 713	3 280	4 489	6 065	7 121
a. 货物差额 Goods Balance	**345**	**340**	**442**	**447**	**590**	**1 342**
贷方 Credit	2 491	2 661	3 257	4 383	5 934	7 625
借方 Debit	2 147	2 321	2 815	3 936	5 344	6 283
b. 服务差额 Services Balance	**−56**	**−59**	**−68**	**−86**	**−97**	**−94**
贷方 Credit	304	333	397	467	624	744
借方 Debit	360	393	465	553	721	838
B. 收益差额 Income Balance	**−147**	**−192**	**−149**	**−78**	**−35**	**−161**
贷方 Credit	126	94	83	161	205	390
借方 Debit	272	286	233	239	241	551
C. 经常转移差额 Current Transfers Balance	**63**	**85**	**130**	**176**	**229**	**254**
贷方 Credit	69	91	138	185	243	277
借方 Debit	5	6	8	8	14	23
二、资本和金融项目差额 Capital and Financial Account Balance	**19**	**348**	**323**	**527**	**1 107**	**1 010**
贷方 Credit	920	995	1 283	2 196	3 434	4 570
借方 Debit	901	648	960	1 669	2 327	3 560
A. 资本账户差额 Capital Account Balance	**−0**	**−1**	**−0**	**−0**	**−1**	**41**
贷方 Credit	—	—	—	—	—	42
借方 Debit	0	1	0	0	1	1
B. 金融账户差额 Financial Account Balance	**20**	**348**	**323**	**528**	**1 107**	**969**
贷方 Credit	920	995	1 283	2 196	3 434	4 529
借方 Debit	900	647	960	1 669	2 326	3 559

单位：亿美元
Unit: USD 100 million

项目 Item	年份 Year	2000	2001	2002	2003	2004	2005
1．直接投资差额 Direct Investment Balance		**375**	**374**	**468**	**472**	**531**	**1 059**
贷方 Credit		421	471	531	555	609	1 242
借方 Debit		46	97	63	83	78	183
2．证券投资差额 Portfolio Investment Balance		**−40**	**−194**	**−103**	**114**	**197**	**−49**
贷方 Credit		78	24	23	123	203	220
借方 Debit		118	218	126	9	6	269
3．其他投资差额 Other Investment Balance		**−315**	**169**	**−41**	**−59**	**379**	**−40**
贷方 Credit		421	501	730	1 518	2 622	3 067
借方 Debit		736	332	771	1 577	2 243	3 108
三、储备资产变动额 Reserve Assets		**−105**	**−473**	**−755**	**−1 379**	**−1 901**	**−2 506**
贷方 Credit		4	—	—	—	5	19
借方 Debit		110	473	755	1 379	1 905	2 526
其中：外汇储备差额 Foreign Exchange Reserves		**−109**	**−466**	**−742**	**−1 377**	**−1 904**	**−2 526**
四、净误差与遗漏 Net Errors and Omissions		**−119**	**−49**	**78**	**393**	**107**	**155**

中国国际收支概览表（5）

China's Balance of Payments Abridged (5)

项目 Item	年份 Year	2006	2007	2008	2009	2010	2011
一、经常项目差额 Current Account Balance		2 327	3 540	4 124	2 611	2 378	2 017
贷方 Credit		11 479	14 679	17 359	14 846	19 355	22 868
借方 Debit		9 152	11 139	13 235	12 235	16 977	20 851
A.货物和服务差额 Goods and Services Balance		2 089	3 075	3 489	2 201	2 230	1 883
贷方 Credit		10 617	13 422	15 817	13 333	17 436	20 867
借方 Debit		8 528	10 347	12 328	11 132	15 206	18 983
a.货物差额 Goods Balance		2 177	3 154	3 607	2 495	2 542	2 435
贷方 Credit		9 697	12 200	14 346	12 038	15 814	19 038
借方 Debit		7 519	9 046	10 739	9 543	13 272	16 603
b.服务差额 Services Balance		−88	−79	−118	−294	−312	−552
贷方 Credit		920	1 222	1 471	1 295	1 622	1 828
借方 Debit		1 008	1 301	1 589	1 589	1 933	2 381
B.收益差额 Income Balance		−54	79	177	73	−259	−119
贷方 Credit		546	830	1 016	1 086	1 424	1 446
借方 Debit		600	752	839	1 013	1 683	1 565
C.经常转移差额 Current Transfers Balance		292	387	458	337	407	253
贷方 Credit		316	426	526	426	495	556
借方 Debit		24	40	68	89	88	303
二、资本和金融项目差额 Capital and Financial Account Balance		526	951	463	1 808	2 869	2 211
贷方 Credit		6 993	9 436	7 972	7 825	11 667	13 982
借方 Debit		6 466	8 485	7 509	6 016	8 798	11 772
A.资本账户差额 Capital Account Balance		40	31	31	40	46	54
贷方 Credit		41	33	33	42	48	56
借方 Debit		1	2	3	2	2	2
B.金融账户差额 Financial Account Balance		486	920	433	1 769	2 822	2 156
贷方 Credit		6 952	9 403	7 939	7 783	11 618	13 926
借方 Debit		6 465	8 482	7 506	6 014	8 796	11 770

单位：亿美元
Unit: USD 100 million

项目 Item	年份 Year	2006	2007	2008	2009	2010	2011
1.直接投资差额 Direct Investment Balance		**1 029**	**1 431**	**1 217**	**703**	**1 857**	**1 704**
贷方 Credit		1 333	1 732	1 904	1 502	2 730	2 717
借方 Debit		304	301	687	799	872	1 012
2.证券投资差额 Portfolio Investment Balance		**−676**	**187**	**427**	**387**	**240**	**196**
贷方 Credit		456	640	677	981	636	519
借方 Debit		1 132	453	250	594	395	323
3.其他投资差额 Other Investment Balance		**133**	**−697**	**−1 211**	**679**	**724**	**255**
贷方 Credit		5 163	7 031	5 358	5 299	8 253	10 690
借方 Debit		5 030	7 728	6 569	4 620	7 528	10 435
三、储备资产变动额 Reserve Assets		**−2 848**	**−4 607**	**−4 795**	**−3 984**	**−4 717**	**−3 878**
贷方 Credit		5	2	—	—	—	10
借方 Debit		2 853	4 609	4 795	3 984	4 717	3 888
其中：外汇储备差额 Foreign Exchange Reserves		−2 853	−4 609	−4 783	−3 821	−4 696	−3 848
四、净误差与遗漏 Net Errors and Omissions		**−6**	**116**	**209**	**−435**	**−529**	**−350**

2011年中国国际收支平衡表

China's Balance of Payments in 2011

项目 Item	差 额 Balance	贷 方 Credit	借 方 Debit
一、经常项目Current Account	2 017	22 868	20 851
A.货物和服务Goods and Services	1 883	20 867	18 983
a.货物Goods	2 435	19 038	16 603
b.服务Services	−552	1 828	2 381
1.运输Transportation	−449	356	804
2.旅游Travel	−241	485	726
3.通讯服务Communication Services	5	17	12
4.建筑服务Construction Services	110	147	37
5.保险服务Insurance Services	−167	30	197
6.金融服务Financial Services	1	8	7
7.计算机和信息服务Computer and Information Services	83	122	38
8.专有权利使用费和特许费Royalties and Licensing Fees	−140	7	147
9.咨询Consulting Service	98	284	186
10.广告、宣传Advertising and Public Opinion Polling	12	40	28
11.电影、音像Audio-visual and Related Services	−3	1	4
12.其他商业服务Other Business Services	140	323	183
13.别处未提及的政府服务Government Services, n.i.e	−3	8	11
B.收益Income	−119	1 446	1 565
1.职工报酬Compensation of Employee	150	166	16
2.投资收益Investment Income	−268	1 280	1 549
C.经常转移Current Transfers	253	556	303
1.各级政府General Government	−26	0	26
2.其他部门Other Sectors	278	556	277
二、资本和金融项目Capital and Financial Account	2 211	13 982	11 772
A.资本项目Capital Account	54	56	2
B.金融项目Financial Account	2 156	13 926	11 770
1.直接投资Direct Investment	1 704	2 717	1 012
1.1 我国在外直接投资Abroad	−497	174	671
1.2 外国在华直接投资In China	2 201	2 543	341
2.证券投资Portfolio Investment	196	519	323
2.1 资产Assets	62	255	192
2.1.1 股本证券Equity Securities	11	112	101
2.1.2 债务证券Debt Securities	51	143	91
2.1.2.1 (中)长期债券Bonds and Notes	50	137	88
2.1.2.2 货币市场工具Money Market Instruments	2	5	4
2.2 负债Liabilities	134	265	131
2.2.1 股本证券Equity Securities	53	152	99
2.2.2 债务证券Debt Securities	81	113	32
2.2.2.1 (中)长期债券Bonds and Notes	30	61	32
2.2.2.2 货币市场工具Money Market Instruments	51	51	0

单位：亿美元
Unit: USD 100 million

项目 Item	差 额 Balance	贷 方 Credit	借 方 Debit
3.其他投资Other Investment	255	10 690	10 435
3.1 资产Assets	−1 668	1 088	2 756
3.1.1 贸易信贷Trade Credits	−710	0	710
长期Long−term	−14	0	14
短期Short−term	−695	0	695
3.1.2 贷款Loans	−453	61	513
长期Long−term	−433	8	441
短期Short−term	−20	53	73
3.1.3 货币和存款Currency and Deposits	−987	501	1 489
3.1.4 其他资产Other Assets	482	526	44
长期Long−term	0	0	0
短期Short−term	482	526	44
3.2 负债Liabilities	1 923	9 602	7 679
3.2.1 贸易信贷Trade Credits	380	454	74
长期Long−term	6	8	1
短期Short−term	374	447	73
3.2.2 贷款Loans	1 051	7 343	6 292
长期Long−term	130	538	408
短期Short−term	920	6 805	5 884
3.2.3 货币和存款Currency and Deposits	483	1 719	1 237
3.2.4 其他负债Other Liabilities	10	86	76
长期Long−term	−15	24	39
短期Short−term	24	61	37
三、 储备资产Reserve Assets	−3 878	10	3 888
3.1 货币黄金Monetary Gold	0	0	0
3.2 特别提款权Special Drawing Rights	5	5	0
3.3 在基金组织的储备头寸Reserve Position in the Fund	−34	6	40
3.4 外汇Foreign Exchange	−3 848	0	3 848
3.5 其他债权Other Claims	0	0	0
四、净误差与遗漏Net Errors and Omissions	−350	0	350

美国国际收支概览表

Balance of Payments Abridged of United States

项目 Item / 年份 Year	2004	2005	2006	2007	2008	2009	2010	2011
一、经常项目差额 Current Account Balance	−628.52	−745.78	−800.63	−710.30	−677.13	−376.55	−470.90	−473.45
贷方 Credit	1 599.21	1 843.74	2 171.04	2 513.26	2 682.20	2 196.55	2 516.91	2 863.25
借方 Debit	2 227.73	2 589.52	2 971.67	3 223.56	3 359.33	2 573.10	2 987.81	3 336.70
A.货物和服务差额 Goods and Services Balance	−605.36	−708.62	−753.29	−696.72	−698.34	−381.27	−500.03	−559.97
贷方 Credit	1 163.14	1 287.44	1 459.82	1 654.56	1 842.68	1 575.04	1 837.58	2 105.04
借方 Debit	1 768.50	1 996.06	2 213.11	2 351.28	2 541.02	1 956.31	2 337.61	2 665.01
a.货物差额 Goods Balance	−660.84	−777.80	−832.90	−815.83	−827.14	−502.54	−642.36	−735.21
贷方 Credit	825.48	915.51	1 043.15	1 168.05	1 311.51	1 073.92	1 293.22	1 501.54
借方 Debit	1 486.32	1 693.31	1 876.05	1 983.88	2 138.65	1 576.46	1 935.58	2 236.75
b.服务差额 Services Balance	55.48	69.18	79.61	119.11	128.80	121.27	142.33	175.24
贷方 Credit	337.66	371.93	416.67	486.51	531.17	501.12	544.36	603.50
借方 Debit	282.18	302.75	337.06	367.40	402.37	379.85	402.03	428.26
B.收益差额 Income Balance	65.08	68.59	44.18	101.48	147.09	128.00	165.22	221.07
贷方 Credit	415.79	537.34	684.62	833.83	813.90	599.50	663.24	738.72
借方 Debit	350.71	468.75	640.44	732.35	666.81	471.50	498.02	517.65
C.经常转移差额 Current Transfers Balance	−88.24	−105.75	−91.52	−115.06	−125.88	−123.28	−136.09	−134.55
贷方 Credit	20.28	18.96	26.60	24.87	25.62	22.01	16.09	19.49
借方 Debit	108.52	124.71	118.12	139.93	151.50	145.29	152.18	154.04
二、资本和金融项目差额 Capital and Financial Account Balance	532.59	699.73	804.99	617.76	741.42	297.94	255.98	408.87
A.资本项目差额 Capital Account Balance	3.05	13.12	−1.79	0.38	6.01	−0.14	−0.15	−1.16

单位：10亿美元
Unit: USD billion

项目　年份 Item　Year	2004	2005	2006	2007	2008	2009	2010	2011
B.金融项目差额 Financial Account Balance	529.54	686.61	806.78	617.38	735.41	298.08	256.13	410.03
1.直接投资差额 Direct Investment Balance	−170.25	76.40	−1.77	−192.87	−18.99	−145.03	−115.12	−178.37
1.1本国对外直接投资差额 Abroad Balance	−316.22	−36.24	−244.92	−414.04	−329.08	−303.61	−351.35	−406.24
1.2外国对内直接投资差额 In United States Balance	145.97	112.64	243.15	221.17	310.09	158.58	236.23	227.87
2.证券投资差额 Portfolio Investment Balance	689.98	574.50	627.84	765.86	803.97	0.23	541.29	145.40
2.1证券投资资产差额 Assets Balance	−177.36	−257.54	−498.90	−390.75	280.29	−359.65	−165.62	−14.65
2.2证券投资负债差额 Liabilities Balance	867.34	832.04	1 126.74	1 156.61	523.68	359.88	706.91	160.05
3.金融衍生工具差额 Financial Derivatives Balance	0	0	29.71	6.22	−32.95	49.46	13.74	6.78
4.其他投资差额 Other Investment Balance	9.81	35.71	151.00	38.17	−16.62	393.42	−183.78	436.22
4.1其他投资资产差额 Assets Balance	−510.09	−266.96	−544.28	−648.69	385.75	576.18	−486.38	40.39
4.2其他投资负债差额 Liabilities Balance	519.90	302.67	695.28	686.86	−402.37	−182.76	302.60	395.83
三、储备资产差额 Reserve Assets Balance	2.80	14.10	2.39	−0.13	−4.84	−52.18	−1.82	−15.98
四、净误差与遗漏 Net Errors and Omissions	93.15	31.94	−6.76	92.66	−59.45	130.79	216.76	80.57

德国国际收支概览表

Balance of Payments Abridged of Germany

项目 Item / 年份 Year	2004	2005	2006	2007	2008	2009	2010	2011
一、经常项目差额 Current Account Balance	127.41	140.21	182.35	248.78	226.28	198.09	200.70	204.23
贷方 Credit	1 244.45	1 367.62	1 600.21	1 930.66	2 069.79	1 680.42	1 824.23	2 116.40
借方 Debit	1 117.04	1 227.41	1 417.86	1 681.88	1 843.51	1 482.33	1 623.53	1 912.17
A.货物和服务差额 Goods and Services Balance	136.77	146.02	162.02	234.18	228.80	162.64	184.85	184.14
贷方 Credit	1 054.83	1 146.59	1 323.76	1 577.12	1 758.82	1 408.22	1 558.76	1 811.92
借方 Debit	918.06	1 000.57	1 161.74	1 342.94	1 530.02	1 245.58	1 373.91	1 627.78
a.货物差额 Goods Balance	187.80	194.90	200.25	273.49	267.23	185.51	208.59	214.55
贷方 Credit	907.79	983.14	1 136.16	1 354.26	1 502.67	1 169.32	1 315	1 547.19
借方 Debit	719.99	788.24	935.91	1 080.77	1 235.44	983.81	1 106.41	1 332.64
b.服务差额 Services Balance	−51.03	−48.88	−38.23	−39.31	−38.43	−22.87	−23.74	−30.41
贷方 Credit	147.04	163.45	187.60	222.86	256.15	238.90	243.76	264.73
借方 Debit	198.07	212.33	225.83	262.17	294.58	261.77	267.50	295.14
B.收益差额 Income Balance	24.67	30.19	55.89	59.06	46.27	81.34	66.81	66.53
贷方 Credit	170.23	200.02	251.69	328.31	283.49	248.27	242.68	276.71
借方 Debit	145.56	169.83	195.8	269.25	237.22	166.93	175.87	210.18
C.经常转移差额 Current Transfers Balance	−34.03	−36.00	−35.56	−44.46	−48.79	−45.89	−50.96	−46.44
贷方 Credit	19.39	21.01	24.76	25.23	27.48	23.93	22.79	27.77
借方 Debit	53.42	57.01	60.32	69.69	76.27	69.82	73.75	74.21
二、资本和金融项目差额 Capital and Financial Account Balance	−152.46	−166.26	−223.70	−289.42	−253.27	−208.46	−195.03	−219.88
A.资本项目差额 Capital Account Balance	0.52	−1.82	−0.34	0.07	−0.18	0.01	−0.75	0.86

单位：10亿美元
Unit: USD billion

项目 Item / 年份 Year	2004	2005	2006	2007	2008	2009	2010	2011
B.金融项目差额 Financial Account Balance	−152.98	−164.44	−223.36	−289.49	−253.09	−208.47	−194.28	−220.74
1.直接投资差额 Direct Investment Balance	−29.76	−30.49	−62.58	−91.14	−68.36	−49.38	−63.57	−13.33
1.1本国对外直接投资差额 Abroad Balance	−19.96	−76.96	−119.22	−171.73	−76.81	−75.06	−110.53	−53.62
1.2外国对内直接投资差额 In Germany Balance	−9.80	46.47	56.64	80.59	8.45	25.68	46.96	40.29
2.证券投资差额 Portfolio Investment Balance	19.25	−35.67	−22.36	215.37	44.54	−113.58	−173.69	55.35
2.1证券投资资产差额 Assets Balance	−128.6	−257.33	−203.39	−198.95	14.74	−106.89	−234.65	−34.85
2.2证券投资负债差额 Liabilities Balance	147.85	221.66	181.03	414.32	29.80	−6.69	60.96	90.20
3.金融衍生工具差额 Financial Derivatives Balance	−9.37	−12.02	−7.77	−119.86	−48.05	13.77	−23.40	−39.92
4.其他投资差额 Other Investment Balance	−133.10	−86.26	−130.65	−293.86	−181.22	−59.28	66.38	−222.84
4.1其他投资资产差额 Assets Balance	−179.47	−161.90	−261.15	−455.26	−221.78	130.59	−170.20	−196.15
4.2其他投资负债差额 Liabilities Balance	46.37	75.64	130.50	161.40	40.56	−189.87	236.58	−26.69
三、储备资产差额 Reserve Assets Balance	1.81	2.60	3.65	−1.23	−2.74	−12.36	−2.13	−3.91
四、净误差与遗漏 Net Errors and Omissions	23.23	23.42	37.69	41.88	29.74	22.73	−3.53	19.54

英国国际收支概览表

Balance of Payments Abridged of United Kingdom

项目 Item / 年份 Year	2004	2005	2006	2007	2008	2009	2010	2011
一、经常项目差额 Current Account Balance	−45.42	−59.40	−81.96	−71.07	−41.16	−37.06	−75.23	−46.03
贷方 Credit	826.97	962.35	1 155.58	1 344.93	1 281.57	891.45	929.55	1 093.69
借方 Debit	872.39	1 021.75	1 237.54	1 416.00	1 322.73	928.51	1 004.78	1 139.72
A.货物和服务差额 Goods and Services Balance	−63.66	−79.88	−79.70	−94.21	−89.31	−54.93	−64.23	−53.32
贷方 Credit	547.38	591.99	684.14	730.57	756.10	595.91	667.60	764.39
借方 Debit	611.04	671.87	763.84	824.78	845.41	650.84	731.83	817.71
a.货物差额 Goods Balance	−111.49	−124.72	−140.66	−179.74	−173.46	−128.56	−152.45	−159.77
贷方 Credit	349.65	384.32	447.59	442.28	468.14	356.35	410.89	479.18
借方 Debit	461.14	509.04	588.25	622.02	641.60	484.91	563.34	638.95
b.服务差额 Services Balance	47.83	44.84	60.96	85.53	84.15	73.63	88.22	106.45
贷方 Credit	197.73	207.67	236.55	288.29	287.96	239.56	256.71	285.21
借方 Debit	149.90	162.83	175.59	202.76	203.81	165.93	168.49	178.76
B.收益差额 Income Balance	37.06	42.11	19.56	50.25	74.64	40.66	20.68	42.72
贷方 Credit	254.37	338.70	437.99	586.56	495.41	269.06	240.13	307.59
借方 Debit	217.31	296.59	418.43	536.31	420.77	228.40	219.45	264.87
C.经常转移差额 Current Transfers Balance	−18.82	−21.63	−21.82	−27.11	−26.49	−22.79	−31.68	−35.43
贷方 Credit	25.22	31.66	33.45	27.80	30.06	26.48	21.82	21.71
借方 Debit	44.04	53.29	55.27	54.91	56.55	49.27	53.50	57.14
二、资本和金融项目差额 Capital and Financial Account Balance	57.60	55.47	79.44	57.69	47.06	76.27	79.40	58.35
A.资本项目差额 Capital Account Balance	3.78	2.83	1.81	5.17	6.05	5.14	5.73	5.75

单位：10亿美元
Unit: USD billion

项目 Item / 年份 Year	2004	2005	2006	2007	2008	2009	2010	2011
B.金融项目差额 Financial Account Balance	53.82	52.64	77.63	52.52	41.01	71.13	73.67	52.60
1.直接投资差额 Direct Investment Balance	-36.62	96.62	68.50	-126.02	-69.64	30.06	23.25	-48.73
1.1本国对外直接投资差额 Abroad Balance	-93.95	-80.79	-85.62	-328.09	-163.15	-42.86	-29.72	-102.99
1.2外国对内直接投资差额 In United Kingdom Balance	57.33	177.41	154.12	202.07	93.51	72.92	52.97	54.26
2.证券投资差额 Portfolio Investment Balance	-81.15	-36.37	26.00	256.13	588.93	38.33	-2.16	-49.07
2.1证券投资资产差额 Assets Balance	-259.45	-273.41	-256.99	-179.74	199.66	-254.61	-122.52	-36.27
2.2证券投资负债差额 Liabilities Balance	178.30	237.04	282.99	435.87	389.27	292.94	120.36	-12.80
3.金融衍生工具差额 Financial Derivatives Balance	-14.27	16.53	40.40	-53.98	-219.23	49.08	49.88	26.83
4.其他投资差额 Other Investment Balance	185.86	-24.14	-57.27	-23.61	-259.05	-46.34	2.70	123.57
4.1其他投资资产差额 Assets Balance	-595.88	-926.19	-708.26	-1 474.38	981.60	507.91	-345.35	-223.68
4.2其他投资负债差额 Liabilities Balance	781.74	902.05	650.99	1 450.77	-1 240.65	-554.25	348.05	347.25
三、储备资产差额 Reserve Assets Balance	-0.41	-1.73	1.30	-2.57	3.07	-9.56	-10.01	-10.87
四、净误差与遗漏 Net Errors and Omissions	-11.78	5.69	1.23	15.96	-8.98	-29.66	5.84	-1.43

巴西国际收支概览表

Balance of Payments Abridged of Japan

项目 Item / 年份 Year	2004	2005	2006	2007	2008	2009	2010	2011
一、经常项目差额 Current Account Balance	**11.74**	**13.98**	**13.62**	**1.55**	**−28.19**	**−24.30**	**−47.32**	**−52.61**
贷方 Credit	115.84	141.60	168.55	201.07	246.22	194.28	245.80	309.95
借方 Debit	104.10	127.62	154.93	199.52	274.41	218.59	293.13	362.57
A.货物和服务差额 Goods and Services Balance	**28.99**	**36.39**	**36.80**	**26.81**	**8.15**	**6.04**	**−10.62**	**−8.11**
贷方 Credit	109.06	134.36	157.27	184.60	228.39	180.72	233.74	294.47
借方 Debit	80.07	97.96	120.47	157.79	220.25	174.68	244.36	302.58
a.货物差额 Goods Balance	**33.67**	**44.70**	**46.46**	**40.03**	**24.84**	**25.29**	**20.15**	**29.80**
贷方 Credit	96.48	118.31	137.81	160.65	197.94	153.00	201.92	256.04
借方 Debit	62.81	73.61	91.35	120.62	173.11	127.71	181.77	226.24
b.服务差额 Services Balance	**−4.68**	**−8.31**	**−9.65**	**−13.22**	**−16.69**	**−19.25**	**−30.77**	**−37.91**
贷方 Credit	12.58	16.05	19.46	23.95	30.45	27.73	31.82	38.43
借方 Debit	17.26	24.36	29.12	37.17	47.14	46.97	62.59	76.34
B.收益差额 Income Balance	**−20.52**	**−25.97**	**−27.49**	**−29.29**	**−40.56**	**−33.68**	**−39.49**	**−47.32**
贷方 Credit	3.20	3.19	6.44	11.49	12.51	8.83	7.41	10.75
借方 Debit	23.72	29.16	33.93	40.78	53.07	42.51	46.89	58.07
C.经常转移差额 Current Transfers Balance	**3.27**	**3.56**	**4.30**	**4.03**	**4.22**	**3.34**	**2.79**	**2.82**
贷方 Credit	3.58	4.05	4.85	4.97	5.32	4.74	4.66	4.73
借方 Debit	0.31	0.49	0.54	0.94	1.09	1.40	1.87	1.91
二、资本和金融项目差额 Capital and Financial Account Balance	**−2.99**	**13.81**	**15.98**	**89.09**	**29.35**	**71.29**	**99.72**	**111.87**
A.资本项目差额 Capital Account Balance	**0.34**	**0.66**	**0.87**	**0.76**	**1.06**	**1.13**	**1.12**	**1.57**

单位：10亿美元
Unit: USD billion

项目 年份 Item Year	2004	2005	2006	2007	2008	2009	2010	2011
B.金融项目差额 Financial Account Balance	-3.33	13.14	15.11	88.33	28.30	70.16	98.60	110.29
1.直接投资差额 Direct Investment Balance	8.69	12.55	-9.42	27.52	24.60	36.03	36.92	75.96
1.1本国对外直接投资差额 Abroad Balance	-9.47	-2.52	-28.20	-7.07	-20.46	10.08	-11.59	9.30
1.2外国对内直接投资差额 In Japan Balance	18.17	15.07	18.78	34.58	45.06	25.95	48.51	66.66
2.证券投资差额 Portfolio Investment Balance	-4.75	4.88	9.57	48.39	1.13	50.28	63.01	25.11
2.1证券投资资产差额 Assets Balance	-0.75	-1.77	0.52	0.29	1.90	4.12	-4.78	7.63
2.2证券投资负债差额 Liabilities Balance	-4.00	6.66	9.05	48.10	-0.77	46.16	67.79	17.47
3.金融衍生工具差额 Financial Derivatives Balance	-0.68	-0.04	0.38	-0.71	-0.31	0.16	-0.11	0.00
4.其他投资差额 Other Investment Balance	-6.60	-4.25	14.58	13.13	2.87	-16.31	-1.22	9.23
4.1其他投资资产差额 Assets Balance	-2.20	-5.03	-8.91	-18.55	-5.27	-30.38	-42.64	-39.91
4.2其他投资负债差额 Liabilities Balance	-4.40	0.78	23.49	31.68	8.14	14.06	41.41	49.14
三、储备资产差额 Reserve Assets Balance	-6.60	-27.57	-30.57	-87.48	-2.97	-47.58	-49.08	-58.63
四、净误差与遗漏 Net Errors and Omissions	-2.14	-0.22	0.97	-3.15	1.81	0.59	-3.31	-0.62

俄罗斯国际收支概览表

Balance of Payments Abridged of Russia

项目 Item / 年份 Year	2004	2005	2006	2007	2008	2009	2010	2011
一、经常项目差额 Current Account Balance	**59.51**	**84.60**	**94.69**	**77.77**	**103.53**	**48.60**	**71.08**	**98.83**
贷方 Credit	219.27	290.73	370.81	449.48	595.53	387.07	492.92	634.77
借方 Debit	159.76	206.13	276.13	371.71	492.00	338.47	421.84	535.94
A.货物和服务差额 Goods and Services Balance	**73.13**	**104.59**	**125.66**	**112.03**	**155.45**	**91.75**	**123.29**	**162.23**
贷方 Credit	203.80	268.77	334.65	393.66	522.78	344.98	445.61	576.04
借方 Debit	130.67	164.18	209.00	281.63	367.33	253.23	322.32	413.80
a.货物差额 Goods Balance	**85.82**	**118.36**	**139.27**	**130.92**	**179.74**	**111.59**	**152.00**	**198.18**
贷方 Credit	183.21	243.80	303.55	354.40	471.60	303.39	400.63	522.01
借方 Debit	97.38	125.43	164.28	223.49	291.86	191.80	248.63	323.83
b.服务差额 Services Balance	**−12.69**	**−13.77**	**−13.61**	**−18.89**	**−24.29**	**−19.84**	**−28.70**	**−35.95**
贷方 Credit	20.59	24.97	31.10	39.26	51.18	41.59	44.98	54.02
借方 Debit	33.29	38.75	44.72	58.14	75.47	61.43	73.68	89.97
B.收益差额 Income Balance	**−12.77**	**−18.95**	**−29.43**	**−30.75**	**−49.16**	**−40.28**	**−48.61**	**−60.21**
贷方 Credit	12.00	17.48	29.76	47.40	61.78	33.18	37.36	42.38
借方 Debit	24.77	36.42	59.19	78.15	110.94	73.47	85.98	102.58
C.经常转移差额 Current Transfers Balance	**−0.85**	**−1.04**	**−1.54**	**−3.51**	**−2.77**	**−2.86**	**−3.60**	**−3.19**
贷方 Credit	3.47	4.49	6.40	8.42	10.97	8.91	9.95	16.36
借方 Debit	4.32	5.53	7.94	11.93	13.73	11.77	13.55	19.55
二、资本和金融项目差额 Capital and Financial Account Balance	**−6.75**	**−11.74**	**3.26**	**84.51**	**−131.18**	**−43.52**	**−26.05**	**−76.21**
A.资本项目差额 Capital Account Balance	**−1.62**	**−12.76**	**0.19**	**−10.22**	**0.50**	**−11.87**	**0.07**	**−0.12**

单位：10亿美元
Unit: USD billion

项目 Item	年份 Year	2004	2005	2006	2007	2008	2009	2010	2011
B.金融项目差额 Financial Account Balance		−5.13	1.02	3.07	94.73	−131.67	−31.65	−26.12	−76.09
1.直接投资差额 Direct Investment Balance		1.66	0.12	6.55	9.16	19.41	−7.17	−9.23	−14.40
1.1本国对外直接投资差额 Abroad Balance		−13.78	−12.77	−23.15	−45.92	−55.59	−43.67	−52.52	−67.28
1.2外国对内直接投资差额 In Russia Balance		15.44	12.89	29.70	55.07	75.00	36.50	43.29	52.88
2.证券投资差额 Portfolio Investment Balance		0.62	−11.38	15.70	5.55	−35.44	−2.18	−1.66	−17.86
2.1证券投资资产差额 Assets Balance		−3.82	−10.67	6.25	−9.99	−7.84	−10.37	−3.47	−10.58
2.2证券投资负债差额 Liabilities Balance		4.44	−0.71	9.45	15.54	−27.59	8.20	1.81	−7.28
3.金融衍生工具差额 Financial Derivatives Balance		−0.10	−0.23	−0.10	0.33	−1.37	−3.24	−1.84	−1.39
4.其他投资差额 Other Investment Balance		−7.31	12.52	−19.08	79.69	−114.28	−19.06	−13.38	−42.43
4.1其他投资资产差额 Assets Balance		−26.64	−33.33	−49.42	−60.06	−177.52	6.14	−23.39	−83.33
4.2其他投资负债差额 Liabilities Balance		19.33	45.85	30.34	139.75	63.24	−25.20	10.01	40.89
三、储备资产差额 Reserve Assets Balance		−46.89	−64.97	−107.47	−148.93	38.92	−3.36	−36.75	−12.64
四、净误差与遗漏 Net Errors and Omissions		−5.87	−7.90	9.52	−13.35	−11.27	−1.72	−8.29	−9.99

南非国际收支概览表

Balance of Payments Abridged of France

项目 | 年份 Item | Year	2004	2005	2006	2007	2008	2009	2010	2011
一、经常项目差额 Current Account Balance	-6.74	-8.52	-13.74	-20.02	-20.08	-11.33	-10.12	-13.68
贷方 Credit	61.71	72.91	85.00	98.23	106.24	83.79	105.60	124.53
借方 Debit	68.45	81.43	98.75	118.25	126.33	95.12	115.72	138.21
A.货物和服务差额 Goods and Services Balance	-0.74	-1.14	-6.22	-7.82	-8.62	-2.25	-0.61	-2.42
贷方 Credit	58.11	67.56	78.04	90.25	98.92	78.56	99.70	117.68
借方 Debit	58.85	68.70	84.26	98.08	107.54	80.82	100.32	120.11
a.货物差额 Goods Balance	-0.28	-0.31	-4.20	-5.16	-4.45	0.53	3.84	2.42
贷方 Credit	48.24	56.26	65.82	76.44	86.12	66.54	85.70	102.86
借方 Debit	48.52	56.57	70.02	81.60	90.57	66.01	81.86	100.44
b.服务差额 Services Balance	-0.46	-0.83	-2.03	-2.66	-4.17	-2.79	-4.45	-4.84
贷方 Credit	9.87	11.30	12.21	13.82	12.81	12.02	14.00	14.82
借方 Debit	10.33	12.13	14.24	16.48	16.98	14.81	18.46	19.66
B.收益差额 Income Balance	-4.32	-4.93	-5.16	-9.84	-9.13	-6.39	-7.22	-9.29
贷方 Credit	3.26	4.64	6.08	6.88	5.94	3.99	4.65	5.30
借方 Debit	7.58	9.57	11.24	16.73	15.08	10.38	11.88	14.59
C.经常转移差额 Current Transfers Balance	-1.69	-2.45	-2.36	-2.35	-2.33	-2.68	-2.28	-1.97
贷方 Credit	0.34	0.71	0.89	1.10	1.38	1.24	1.25	1.54
借方 Debit	2.03	3.16	3.25	3.45	3.71	3.93	3.53	3.51
二、资本和金融项目差额 Capital and Financial Account Balance	7.45	12.64	15.37	20.74	11.78	16.30	8.87	10.98
A.资本项目差额 Capital Account Balance	0.05	0.03	0.03	0.03	0.03	0.03	0.03	0.03

单位：10亿美元
Unit: USD billion

项目 Item	年份 Year	2004	2005	2006	2007	2008	2009	2010	2011
B.金融项目差额 Financial Account Balance		**7.40**	**12.61**	**15.34**	**20.71**	**11.76**	**16.28**	**8.84**	**10.94**
1.直接投资差额 Direct Investment Balance		**−0.60**	**5.61**	**−6.11**	**2.75**	**11.76**	**4.04**	**1.39**	**6.22**
1.1本国对外直接投资差额 Abroad Balance		−1.31	−0.91	−5.93	−2.98	2.12	−1.31	0.16	0.50
1.2外国对内直接投资差额 In France Balance		0.70	6.52	−0.18	5.74	9.64	5.35	1.22	5.72
2.证券投资差额 Portfolio Investment Balance		**6.36**	**4.81**	**19.63**	**10.24**	**−14.30**	**11.62**	**9.77**	**0.37**
2.1证券投资资产差额 Assets Balance		−0.95	−0.91	−2.23	−3.44	−6.72	−1.75	−4.61	−6.31
2.2证券投资负债差额 Liabilities Balance		7.31	5.72	21.86	13.68	−7.58	13.37	14.39	6.68
3.金融衍生工具差额 Financial Derivatives Balance		**0.00**	**0.00**	**0.00**	**0.00**	**0.00**	**0.00**	**0.00**	**0.00**
4.其他投资差额 Other Investment Balance		**1.64**	**2.19**	**1.82**	**7.71**	**14.29**	**0.61**	**−2.32**	**4.36**
4.1其他投资资产差额 Assets Balance		−0.43	−3.62	−6.63	0.52	8.92	3.10	−3.22	−0.06
4.2其他投资负债差额 Liabilities Balance		2.07	5.81	8.46	7.20	5.37	−2.49	0.89	4.42
三、储备资产差额 Reserve Assets Balance		**−6.32**	**−5.77**	**−3.71**	**−5.74**	**−2.23**	**−4.17**	**−3.80**	**−4.71**
四、净误差与遗漏 Net Errors and Omissions		**5.62**	**1.64**	**2.09**	**5.02**	**10.53**	**−0.80**	**5.05**	**7.41**

韩国国际收支概览表

Balance of Payments Abridged of Korea

项目 Item / 年份 Year	2004	2005	2006	2007	2008	2009	2010	2011
一、经常项目差额 Current Account Balance	32.31	18.61	14.08	21.77	3.20	32.79	28.21	26.51
贷方 Credit	323.20	359.80	417.01	492.64	561.01	458.98	576.28	680.33
借方 Debit	290.89	341.19	402.93	470.87	557.81	426.19	548.07	653.83
A.货物和服务差额 Goods and Services Balance	33.70	22.91	18.10	25.16	−0.56	31.23	30.67	26.57
贷方 Credit	304.68	339.62	393.34	462.56	525.29	431.77	547.01	647.56
借方 Debit	270.98	316.71	375.24	437.40	525.85	400.55	516.33	620.99
a.货物差额 Goods Balance	39.68	32.84	31.50	37.18	5.17	37.86	41.88	31.15
贷方 Credit	260.24	289.89	336.58	389.65	434.70	358.22	464.30	552.80
借方 Debit	220.57	257.05	305.08	352.47	429.53	320.36	422.43	521.64
b.服务差额 Services Balance	−5.97	−9.93	−13.40	−12.01	−5.74	−6.64	−11.20	−4.58
贷方 Credit	44.44	49.73	56.76	72.92	90.59	73.55	82.71	94.77
借方 Debit	50.41	59.66	70.16	84.93	96.33	80.19	93.91	99.35
B.收益差额 Income Balance	1.04	−1.82	0.07	0.13	4.44	2.28	0.77	2.46
贷方 Credit	9.37	10.18	14.09	18.91	21.65	14.51	15.88	17.42
借方 Debit	8.33	11.99	14.01	18.78	17.22	12.24	15.11	14.97
C.经常转移差额 Current Transfers Balance	−2.43	−2.48	−4.09	−3.53	−0.67	−0.71	−3.23	−2.52
贷方 Credit	9.15	10.00	9.59	11.16	14.07	12.70	13.40	15.35
借方 Debit	11.58	12.49	13.68	14.69	14.74	13.41	16.63	17.87
二、资本和金融项目差额 Capital and Financial Account Balance	3.24	0.28	7.96	−8.75	−57.60	34.06	1.76	−18.05
A.资本项目差额 Capital Account Balance	−1.75	−2.34	−3.13	−2.39	0.11	0.29	−0.17	0.15

单位：10亿美元
Unit: USD billion

项目 Item ｜ 年份 Year	2004	2005	2006	2007	2008	2009	2010	2011
B.金融项目差额 Financial Account Balance	5.00	2.62	11.09	−6.36	−57.71	33.77	1.94	−18.20
1.直接投资差额 Direct Investment Balance	3.60	−0.06	−7.59	−17.94	−16.94	−14.95	−19.38	−15.69
1.1本国对外直接投资差额 Abroad Balance	−5.65	−6.37	−11.17	−19.72	−20.25	−17.20	−19.23	−20.35
1.2外国对内直接投资差额 In Korea Balance	9.25	6.31	3.59	1.78	3.31	2.25	−0.15	4.66
2.证券投资差额 Portfolio Investment Balance	6.60	−3.52	−23.23	−26.06	−2.41	49.73	38.55	10.31
2.1证券投资资产差额 Assets Balance	−11.78	−17.63	−31.29	−56.44	23.48	1.44	−3.54	−5.23
2.2证券投资负债差额 Liabilities Balance	18.37	14.11	8.06	30.38	−25.89	48.29	42.09	15.54
3.金融衍生工具差额 Financial Derivatives Balance	2.02	1.79	0.48	5.44	−14.77	−3.09	−0.01	−1.74
4.其他投资差额 Other Investment Balance	−7.22	4.40	41.42	32.19	−23.59	2.08	−17.23	−11.09
4.1其他投资资产差额 Assets Balance	−8.14	−2.66	−7.95	−14.84	−13.74	1.69	−12.26	−23.62
4.2其他投资负债差额 Liabilities Balance	0.92	7.06	49.37	47.02	−9.85	0.39	−4.97	12.53
三、储备资产差额 Reserve Assets Balance	−38.68	−19.86	−22.09	−15.11	56.45	−68.65	−27.17	−13.98
四、净误差与遗漏 Net Errors and Omissions	3.12	0.98	0.05	2.09	−2.04	1.80	−2.80	5.53

中国国际投资头寸表

China's International Investment Position

项目 Item	2005年末 End-2005	2006年末 End-2006	2007年末 End-2007	2008年末 End-2008	2009年末 End-2009	2010年末 End-2010	2011年末 End-2011
净头寸Net	4 077	6 402	11 881	14 938	14 905	16 880	17 747
A.资产Assets	12 233	16 905	24 162	29 567	34 369	41 189	47 182
1.在国外直接投资Direct Investment Abroad	645	906	1 160	1 857	2 458	3 172	3 642
2.证券投资Portfolio Investment	1 167	2 652	2 846	2 525	2 428	2 571	2 600
2.1股本证券Equity Securities	0	15	196	214	546	630	619
2.2债务证券Debt Securities	1 167	2 637	2 650	2 311	1 882	1 941	1 981
3.其他投资Other Investment	2 164	2 539	4 683	5 523	4 952	6 304	8 382
3.1贸易信贷Trade Credits	661	922	1 160	1 102	1 444	2 060	2 769
3.2贷款Loans	719	670	888	1 071	974	1 174	2 232
3.3货币和存款Currency and Deposits	675	736	1 380	1 529	1 310	2 051	2 829
3.4其他资产Other Assets	109	210	1 255	1 821	1 224	1 018	552
4.储备资产Reserve Assets	8 257	10 808	15 473	19 662	24 532	29 142	32 558
4.1货币黄金Monetary Gold	42	123	170	169	371	481	530
4.2特别提款权Special Drawing Right	12	11	12	12	125	123	119
4.3在基金组织中的储备头寸Reserve Position in the Fund	14	11	8	20	44	64	98
4.4外汇Foreign Exchange	8 189	10 663	15 282	19 460	23 992	28 473	31 811

单位：亿美元
Unit: USD 100 million

项目 Item	2005年末 End-2005	2006年末 End-2006	2007年末 End-2007	2008年末 End-2008	2009年末 End-2009	2010年末 End-2010	2011年末 End-2011
B.负债Liabilities	8 156	10 503	12 281	14 629	19 464	24 308	29 434
1.外国来华直接投资 Direct Investment in Reporting Economy	4 715	6 144	7 037	9 155	13 148	15 696	18 042
2.证券投资 Portfolio Investment	766	1 207	1 466	1 677	1 900	2 239	2 485
2.1股本证券Equity Securities	636	1 065	1 290	1 505	1 748	2 061	2 114
2.2债务证券Debt Securities	130	142	176	172	152	178	371
3.其他投资 Other Investment	2 675	3 152	3 778	3 796	4 416	6 373	8 907
3.1贸易信贷Trade Credits	1 063	1 196	1 487	1 296	1 617	2 112	2 492
3.2贷款Loans	870	985	1 033	1 030	1 636	2 389	3 724
3.3货币和存款Currency and Deposits	484	595	791	918	937	1 650	2 477
3.4其他负债Other Liabilities	257	377	467	552	227	222	214

外汇储备

Foreign Exchange Reserves

单位：亿美元
Unit: USD 100 million

年份 Year	外汇储备余额 Foreign Exchange Reserves	外汇储备增加额 Increase of Foreign Exchange Reserves
1990	111	55
1991	217	106
1992	194	−23
1993	212	18
1994	516	304
1995	736	220
1996	1 050	315
1997	1 399	348
1998	1 450	51
1999	1 547	97
2000	1 656	109
2001	2 122	466
2002	2 864	742
2003	4 033	1 168
2004	6 099	2 067
2005	8 189	2 090
2006	10 663	2 475
2007	15 282	4 619
2008	19 460	4 178
2009	23 992	4 531
2010	28 473	4 481
2011	31 811	3 338

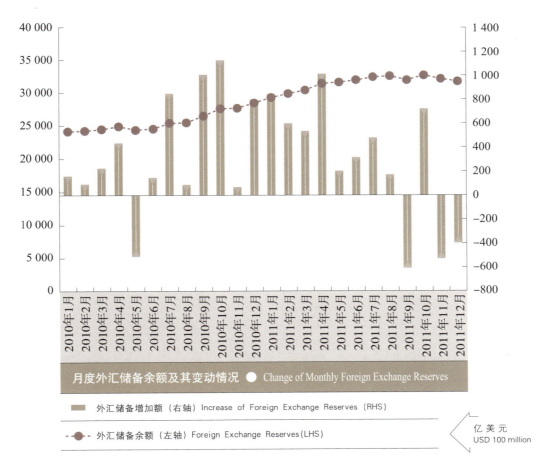

月度外汇储备余额及其变动情况 ● Change of Monthly Foreign Exchange Reserves

■ 外汇储备增加额（右轴）Increase of Foreign Exchange Reserves（RHS）

- -●- 外汇储备余额（左轴）Foreign Exchange Reserves（LHS）

亿 美 元
USD 100 million

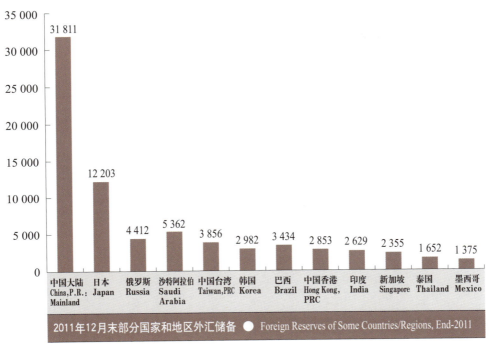

2011年12月末部分国家和地区外汇储备 ● Foreign Reserves of Some Countries/Regions, End-2011

亿 美 元
USD 100 million

二、对外贸易[①]

II. Foreign Trade

2011年世界货物贸易出口前十名

Top 10 Countries/Regions of Goods Export in 2011

国家/地区 Countries/Regions	出口额（10亿美元） Export（USD billion）	增长 Increase（%）	占世界出口总额比重 Ratio to total Export of the World（%）	2010年排名 Ranking in 2010
世界World	18 215	15	100	
1.中国PRC	1 899	20	10.4	1
2.美国USA	1 481	16	8.1	2
3.德国Germany	1 474	17	8.1	3
4.日本Japan	823	7	4.5	4
5.荷兰Netherlands	660	15	3.6	5
6.法国France	597	14	3.3	6
7.韩国Korea	555	19	3.0	7
8.意大利Italy	523	17	2.9	8
9.俄罗斯Russia	522	30	2.9	12
10.比利时Belgium	476	17	2.6	9

① 数据来源：海关总署；世界贸易组织。
Sources：General Administration of Customs；World Trade Organization.

2011年世界货物贸易进口前十名

国家/地区 Countries/Regions	进口额（10亿美元） Import（USD billion）	增长 Increase（%）	占世界进口总额比重 Ratio to total Import of the World（%）	2010年排名 Ranking in 2010
世界World	18 380	19	100	
1.美国USA	2 265	15	12.3	1
2.中国PRC	1 743	25	9.5	2
3.德国Germany	1 254	19	6.8	3
4.日本Japan	854	23	4.6	5
5.法国France	714	17	3.9	4
6.英国UK	636	13	3.5	6
7.荷兰Netherlands	597	16	3.2	7
8.意大利Italy	557	14	3.0	8
9.韩国Korea	525	23	2.9	10
10.中国香港Hong Kong,PRC	511	16	2.8	9

中国进出口总值

单位：亿美元
Unit: USD 100 million

China's Total Value of Import & Export

年度 Year	进出口 Import & Export	出口 Export	进口 Import	差额 Balance
1981	440	220	220	0
1982	416	223	193	30
1983	436	222	214	8
1984	535	261	274	−13
1985	696	274	423	−149
1986	738	309	429	−120
1987	827	394	432	−38
1988	1 028	475	553	−78
1989	1 117	525	591	−66
1990	1 154	621	534	87
1991	1 357	719	638	81
1992	1 655	849	806	44
1993	1 957	917	1 040	−122
1994	2 366	1 210	1 156	54
1995	2 809	1 488	1 321	167
1996	2 899	1 511	1 388	122
1997	3 252	1 828	1 424	404
1998	3 239	1 837	1 402	435
1999	3 606	1 949	1 657	292
2000	4 743	2 492	2 251	241
2001	5 097	2 661	2 436	226
2002	6 208	3 256	2 952	304
2003	8 510	4 382	4 128	255
2004	11 546	5 933	5 612	321
2005	14 219	7 620	6 600	1 020
2006	17 604	9 689	7 915	1 775
2007	21 766	12 205	9 561	2 643
2008	25 633	14 307	11 326	2 981
2009	22 072	12 017	10 059	1 957
2010	29 728	15 779	13 948	1 831
2011	36 421	18 986	17 435	1 551

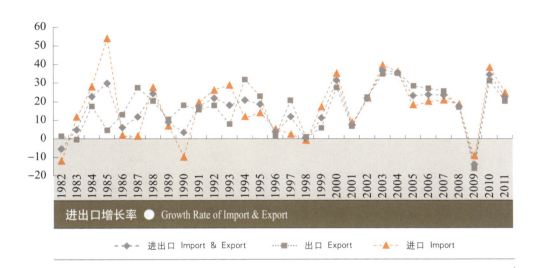

进出口增长率　● Growth Rate of Import & Export

- ◆ - 进出口 Import & Export　- ■ - 出口 Export　- ▲ - 进口 Import

增长率 (%)
Growth Rate (%)

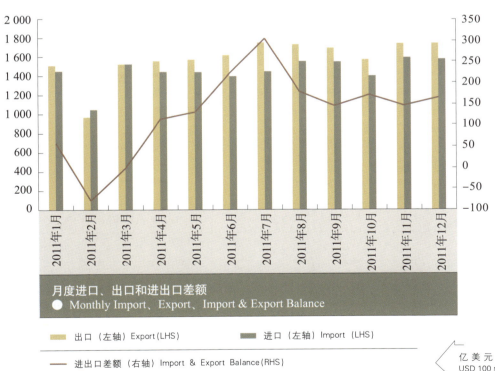

月度进口、出口和进出口差额
● Monthly Import、Export、Import & Export Balance

出口（左轴）Export (LHS)　进口（左轴）Import (LHS)

进出口差额（右轴）Import & Export Balance (RHS)

亿美元
USD 100 million

按贸易方式分类进出口

Import & Export by Trading Forms

贸易方式 Trading Forms	2003	2004	2005	2006	2007	2008	2009	2010	2011
进口 Import	412 836	561 423	660 118	791 614	955 818	1 133 086	1 005 555	1 394 829	174 3458
一般贸易 Ordinary Trade	187 700	248 227	279 719	333 181	428 648	572 677	533 872	767 978	1 007 464
国家间、国际组织间无偿援助和捐赠的物资 Foreign Aid and Donation by Overseas	114	98	49	65	35	49	43	22	16
其他捐赠物资 Other Donations	21	12	19	22	10	58	136	185	266
来料加工装配贸易 Processing and Assembling Trade	39 125	53 721	67 029	73 834	89 165	90 162	75 993	99 295	93 635
进料加工贸易 Processing with Imported Materials	123 810	168 020	206 997	247 662	279 228	288 243	246 345	318 134	376 161
寄售代销贸易 Goods on Consignment	6	8	6	3	2	2	2	2	2
边境小额贸易 Border Trade	4 303	5 043	5 721	6 214	7 589	8 975	7 196	9 634	14 448
加工贸易进口设备 Equipment Imported for Processing & Assembling	1 961	2 603	2 862	2 817	3 277	2 859	953	1 212	885
租赁贸易 Goods on Lease	1 392	2 223	3 681	8 067	8 280	6 932	3 448	5 628	5 459
外商投资企业作为投资进口的设备物品 Equipment or Materials Imported as Investment by Foreign-invested Enterprises	20 968	31 203	27 674	27 823	25 906	27 677	15 176	16 312	17 508
出料加工贸易 Outward Processing Trade	23	24	33	33	39	160	78	126	73
易货贸易 Barter Trade	6	13	3	6	4	1	8	1	2
免税外汇商品 Duty Free Commodities on Payment of Foreign Exchange	7	6	8	6	6	6	5	10	13
保税仓库进出境货物 Customs Warehousing Trade	7 185	11 081	20 065	32 018	41 720	57 277	54 392	61 099	79 658
保税仓储转口货物 Entrepot Trade by Bonded Area	25 147	37 720	44 255	55 508	66 910	73 739	64 259	109 241	140 831
出口加工区进口设备 Equipment Imported into Export Processing Zone	558	882	1 411	3 623	4 108	3 118	2 113	3 994	4 741
其他 Others	510	539	586	732	890	1 150	1 535	1 957	2 296

单位：百万美元
Unit: USD million

贸易方式 Trading Forms	2003	2004	2005	2006	2007	2008	2009	2010	2011
出口 Export	438 371	593 368	761 999	969 073	1 218 015	1 428 546	1 201 663	1 577 932	1 898 600
一般贸易 Ordinary Trade	182 034	243 635	315 091	416 318	538 576	662 584	529 833	720 733	917 124
国家间、国际组织间无偿援助和捐赠的物资 Foreign Aid and Donation by Overseas	106	187	225	211	201	231	291	294	471
其他捐赠物资 Other Donations	0	0	0	0	0	2	8	3	11
补偿贸易 Compensation Trade	17	9	0	1	0	0	0	0	0
来料加工装配贸易 Processing and Assembling Trade	54 332	68 569	83 970	94 483	116 043	110 520	93 423	112 317	107 653
进料加工贸易 Processing with Imported Materials	187 517	259 419	332 511	415 892	501 613	564 663	493 558	628 017	727 763
寄售代销贸易 Goods on Consignment	1	1	1	2	4	4	6	1	2
边境小额贸易 Border Trade	3 476	4 431	7 409	9 943	13 739	21 904	13 667	16 408	20 203
对外承包工程出口货物 Contracting Projects	640	1 130	1 705	3 071	5 188	10 963	13 357	12 617	14 923
租赁贸易 Goods on Lease	8	15	90	214	84	189	117	145	166
出料加工贸易 Outward Processing Trade	20	27	27	24	44	118	46	185	198
易货贸易 Barter Trade	41	28	17	19	48	16	1	1	1
保税仓库进出境货物 Customs Warehousing Trade	4 017	5 739	7 956	13 069	18 624	28 404	26 793	35 366	43 294
保税仓储转口货物 Entrepot Trade by Bonded Area	5 488	9 354	11 615	14 463	20 977	23 937	21 476	36 502	49 655
其他 Others	674	824	1 380	1 361	2 916	5 011	9 088	15 343	17 135

按企业类型分类进出口

Import & Export by Type of Enterprises

企业类型Type of Enterprises	2003	2004	2005	2006	2007	2008	2009	2010	2011
进口Import	**4 128**	**5 614**	**6 601**	**7 916**	**9 558**	**11 331**	**10 056**	**13 948**	**17 435**
国有企业 State-owned Enterprises	1 425	1 765	1 972	2 252	2 697	3 538	2 885	3 876	4 934
外商投资企业 Foreign-funded Enterprises	2 319	3 246	3 875	4 726	5 594	6 200	5 452	7 380	8 648
中外合作 Sino-foreign Contractual Joint Ventures	100	107	96	99	88	88	66	74	86
中外合资 Sino-foreign Equity Joint Ventures	809	1 092	1 184	1 356	1 549	1 818	1 586	2 095	2 561
外商独资 Foreign Investment Enterprises	1 411	2 046	2 595	3 270	3 957	4 294	3 799	5 212	6 002
集体企业 Collective Enterprises	132	177	205	200	232	289	265	349	407
其他 Other Enterprises	252	427	549	738	1 035	1 304	1 454	2 343	3 445
出口Export	**4 384**	**5 934**	**7 620**	**9 691**	**12 180**	**14 285**	**12 017**	**15 779**	**18 986**
国有企业 State-owned Enterprises	1 380	1 536	1 688	1 913	2 248	2 572	1 910	2 344	2 672
外商投资企业 Foreign-funded Enterprises	2 403	3 386	4 442	5 638	6 955	7 906	6 722	8 623	9 953
中外合作 Sino-foreign Contractual Joint Ventures	132	148	157	177	181	183	146	165	177
中外合资 Sino-foreign Equity Joint Ventures	810	1 096	1 360	1 638	1 988	2 269	1 824	2 376	2 731
外商独资 Foreign Investment Enterprises	1 461	2 142	2 925	3 824	4 786	5 454	4 752	6 082	7 046
集体企业 Collective Enterprises	251	318	365	411	469	547	405	499	554
其他 Other Enterprises	349	694	1 125	1 728	2 508	3 260	2 979	4 314	5 807
差额Balance	**255**	**319**	**1 019**	**1 775**	**2 622**	**2 955**	**1 961**	**1 831**	**1 551**
国有企业 State-owned Enterprises	−44	−229	−284	−339	−449	−966	−975	−1 532	−2 262
外商投资企业 Foreign-funded Enterprises	84	140	567	912	1 361	1 706	1 270	1 243	1 305
中外合作 Sino-foreign Contractual Joint Ventures	33	40	61	78	93	95	80	91	91
中外合资 Sino-foreign Equity Joint Ventures	2	4	176	281	439	451	238	281	170
外商独资 Foreign Investment Enterprises	50	96	330	553	829	1 160	953	870	1 044
集体企业 Collective Enterprises	119	141	160	211	237	258	140	150	147
其他 Other Enterprises	97	267	576	990	1 473	1 956	1 525	1 971	2 362

2011年按贸易方式分类的进口构成
Components of Import by Trading Forms in 2011

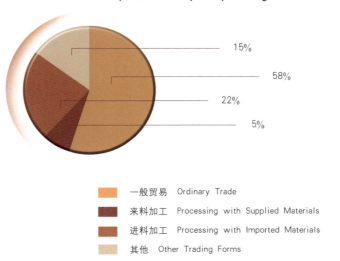

15%

58%

22%

5%

一般贸易　Ordinary Trade

来料加工　Processing with Supplied Materials

进料加工　Processing with Imported Materials

其他　Other Trading Forms

2011年按贸易方式分类的出口构成
Components of Export by Trading Forms in 2011

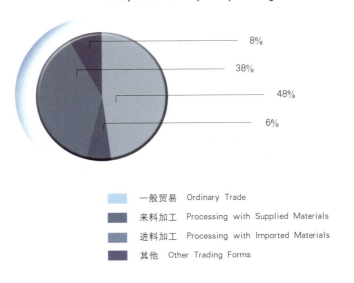

8%

38%

48%

6%

一般贸易　Ordinary Trade

来料加工　Processing with Supplied Materials

进料加工　Processing with Imported Materials

其他　Other Trading Forms

2011年按企业类型分类的进口构成
Components of Import by Type of Enterprises in 2011

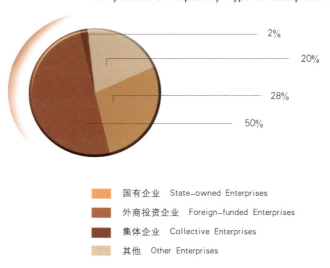

2%
20%
28%
50%

■ 国有企业　State-owned Enterprises
■ 外商投资企业　Foreign-funded Enterprises
■ 集体企业　Collective Enterprises
■ 其他　Other Enterprises

2011年按企业类型分类的出口构成
Components of Export by Type of Enterprises in 2011

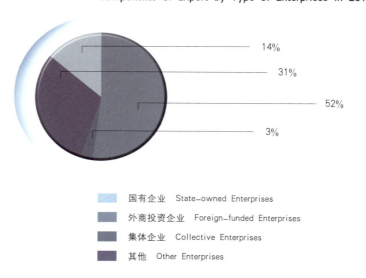

14%
31%
52%
3%

■ 国有企业　State-owned Enterprises
■ 外商投资企业　Foreign-funded Enterprises
■ 集体企业　Collective Enterprises
■ 其他　Other Enterprises

2011年进出口按贸易方式分类

Import & Export by Trading Forms in 2011

单位：亿美元
Unit: USD 100 million

贸易方式 Trading Forms	进口 金额Value	Import 同比(%)Increase	出口 金额Value	Export 同比(%)Increase	进出口差额 Import & Export Balance
总值 **Total Value**	**17 435**	**24.9**	**18 986**	**20.3**	**1 551**
一般贸易 Ordinary Trade	10 075	31	9 171	27.3	−904
加工贸易 Processing Trade	4 698	12.6	8 355	12.9	3 657
来料加工 With Supplied Material	936	−5.8	1 077	−4.1	141
进料加工 With Imported Material	3 762	18.3	7 278	15.9	3 516
其他贸易 Other Trading Forms	2 662	27.1	1 460	24.9	−1 202

2011年进出口按企业类型分类

Import & Export by Type of Enterprises in 2011

单位：亿美元
Unit: USD 100 million

企业类型　Type of Enterprises	进口 金额Value	Import 同比(%)Increase	出口 金额Value	Export 同比(%)Increase	进出口差额 Import & Export Balance
总值 **Total Value**	**17 435**	**24.9**	**18 986**	**20.3**	**1 551**
国有企业 State-owned Enterprises	4 934	27.1	2 672	14.1	-2 262
外资企业 Foreign-funded Enterprises	8 648	17.1	9 953	15.4	1 305
集体企业 Collective Enterprises	407	16.4	554	11.1	147
其他企业 Other Enterprises	3 445	46.8	5 807	34.6	2 362

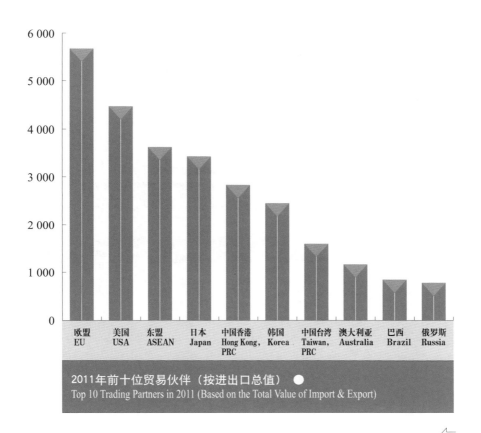

2011年前十位贸易顺差来源地 ● Top 10 Sources of Trade Surplus in 2011

亿美元
USD 100 million

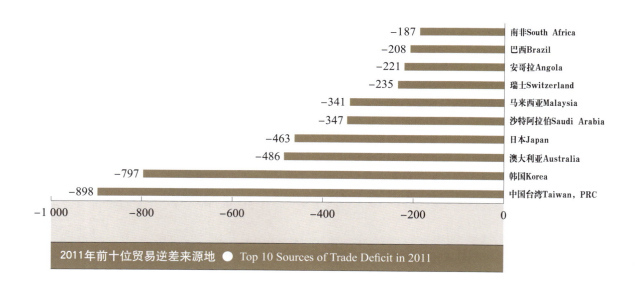

2011年前十位贸易逆差来源地 ● Top 10 Sources of Trade Deficit in 2011

亿美元
USD 100 million

三、外汇市场和人民币汇率[①]

III. Foreign Exchange Market and Exchange Rate of RMB

人民币对美元交易中间价月平均汇价

人民币元/100美元
RMB per 100 USD

Monthly Average Transaction Mid Rates of RMB against USD, 1980—2010

月份 Month	1980年	1981年	1982年	1983年	1984年	1985年	1986年	1987年	1988年	1989年
1 月/Jan	149.37	154.87	176.77	192.01	204.12	280.88	320.15	372.21	372.21	372.21
2 月/Feb	150.05	161.06	181.74	196.03	205.72	282.51	320.70	372.21	372.21	372.21
3 月/Mar	155.12	162.80	183.79	197.80	206.08	284.51	321.20	372.21	372.21	372.21
4 月/Apr	155.70	166.20	185.19	198.72	208.91	284.11	320.61	372.21	372.21	372.21
5 月/May	149.06	172.27	180.97	198.52	218.21	284.75	319.44	372.21	372.21	372.21
6 月/Jun	146.50	176.05	189.70	198.95	221.22	286.25	320.35	372.21	372.21	372.21
7 月/Jul	145.25	175.98	192.36	198.88	229.39	287.38	363.82	372.21	372.21	372.21
8 月/Aug	147.26	179.52	193.87	198.00	236.43	290.23	370.36	372.21	372.21	372.21
9 月/Sep	146.81	175.01	195.04	198.14	253.26	296.26	370.66	372.21	372.21	372.21
10 月/Oct	148.03	175.05	198.22	196.17	264.00	306.73	371.64	372.21	372.21	372.21
11月/Nov	151.73	173.46	199.41	198.90	266.16	320.15	372.21	372.21	372.21	372.21
12月/Dec	154.19	173.78	193.99	198.69	278.91	320.15	372.21	372.21	372.21	423.82
年平均 Annual Average	149.84	170.50	189.25	197.57	232.70	293.66	345.28	372.21	372.21	376.51

①资料来源：国家外汇管理局。
Sources：State Administration of Foreign Exchange.

人民币对美元交易中间价月平均汇价

Monthly Average Transaction Mid Rates of RMB against USD, 1980—2011

月份 Month	1990年	1991年	1992年	1993年	1994年	1995年	1996年	1997年	1998年	1999年	2000年
1月/Jan	472.21	522.21	544.81	576.40	870.00	844.13	831.86	829.63	827.91	827.90	827.93
2月/Feb	472.21	522.21	546.35	576.99	870.28	843.54	831.32	829.29	827.91	827.80	827.79
3月/Mar	472.21	522.21	547.34	573.13	870.23	842.76	832.89	829.57	827.92	827.91	827.86
4月/Apr	472.21	526.59	549.65	570.63	869.55	842.25	833.15	829.57	827.92	827.92	827.93
5月/May	472.21	531.39	550.36	572.17	866.49	831.28	832.88	829.29	827.90	827.85	827.77
6月/Jun	472.21	535.35	547.51	573.74	865.72	830.08	832.26	829.21	827.97	827.80	827.72
7月/Jul	472.21	535.55	544.32	576.12	864.03	830.07	831.60	829.11	827.98	827.77	827.93
8月/Aug	472.21	537.35	542.87	577.64	858.98	830.75	830.81	828.94	827.99	827.73	827.96
9月/Sep	472.21	537.35	549.48	578.70	854.03	831.88	830.44	828.72	827.89	827.74	827.86
10月/Oct	472.21	537.90	553.69	578.68	852.93	831.55	830.00	828.38	827.78	827.74	827.85
11月/Nov	495.54	538.58	561.31	579.47	851.69	831.35	829.93	828.11	827.78	827.82	827.74
12月/Dec	522.21	541.31	579.82	580.68	848.45	831.56	829.90	827.96	827.79	827.93	827.72
年平均 Annual Average	478.32	532.33	551.46	576.20	861.87	835.10	831.42	828.98	827.91	827.83	827.84

人民币元/100美元
RMB per 100 USD

月份 Month	2001年	2002年	2003年	2004年	2005年	2006年	2007年	2008年	2009年	2010年	2011年
1 月/Jan	827.71	827.67	827.68	827.69	827.65	806.68	778.98	724.78	683.82	682.73	660.27
2 月/Feb	827.70	827.66	827.73	827.71	827.65	804.93	775.46	716.01	683.57	682.70	658.31
3 月/Mar	827.76	827.70	827.72	827.71	827.65	803.50	773.90	707.52	683.41	682.64	656.62
4 月/Apr	827.71	827.72	827.71	827.69	827.65	801.56	772.47	700.07	683.12	682.62	652.92
5 月/May	827.72	827.69	827.69	827.71	827.65	801.52	767.04	697.24	682.45	682.74	649.88
6 月/Jun	827.71	827.70	827.71	827.67	827.65	800.67	763.30	689.71	683.32	681.65	647.78
7 月/Jul	827.69	827.68	827.73	827.67	822.90	799.10	758.05	683.76	683.20	677.75	646.14
8 月/Aug	827.70	827.67	827.70	827.68	810.19	797.33	757.53	685.15	683.22	679.01	640.90
9 月/Sep	827.68	827.70	827.71	827.67	809.22	793.68	752.58	683.07	682.89	674.62	638.33
10 月/Oct	827.68	827.69	827.67	827.65	808.89	790.32	750.12	683.16	682.75	667.32	635.66
11 月/Nov	827.69	827.71	827.69	827.65	808.40	786.52	742.33	682.86	682.74	665.58	634.08
12月/Dec	827.68	827.72	827.70	827.65	807.59	782.38	736.76	684.24	682.79	665.15	632.81
年平均 Annual Average	827.70	827.70	827.70	827.68	819.42	797.18	760.40	694.51	683.10	676.95	646.14

2011年1-12月人民币市场汇率汇总表

Transaction Mid Rates of RMB in 2011

月份 Month	币种 Currency	期初价 Beginning of Period	期末价 End of Period	最高价 Highest	最低价 Lowest	期平均 Period Average	累计平均 Accumulative Average
1月 Jan	美元 USD	662.15	658.91	663.49	658.76	660.27	660.27
	欧元 EUR	883.01	895.52	905.05	855.67	881.27	881.27
	日元 JPY	8.0977	8.0223	8.0977	7.9390	7.9868	7.9868
	港币 HKD	85.213	84.560	85.353	84.506	84.872	84.872
	英镑 GBP	1 025.27	1 043.71	1 053.20	1 025.27	1 041.22	1 041.22
	林吉特 MYR	46.326	46.427	47.558	46.242	46.418	46.418
	卢布 RUB	461.34	452.35	463.33	449.32	456.64	456.64
2月 Feb	美元 USD	658.60	657.52	659.85	657.05	658.31	659.43
	欧元 EUR	903.50	902.05	907.94	889.54	898.38	888.60
	日元 JPY	8.0214	8.0460	8.0460	7.8661	7.9494	7.9707
	港币 HKD	84.482	84.363	84.666	84.363	84.501	84.713
	英镑 GBP	1 057.55	1 057.49	1 068.45	1 057.49	1 061.41	1 049.87
	林吉特 MYR	46.343	46.472	46.495	46.048	46.286	46.361
	卢布 RUB	451.45	440.18	451.45	440.18	444.15	451.29
3月 Mar	美元 USD	657.06	655.64	657.50	655.64	656.62	658.32
	欧元 EUR	908.19	926.81	932.98	905.35	919.21	900.74
	日元 JPY	8.0222	7.8883	8.2743	7.8883	8.0326	7.9953
	港币 HKD	84.366	84.225	84.405	84.123	84.260	84.533
	英镑 GBP	1 070.19	1 055.35	1 073.13	1 049.57	1 061.56	1 054.51
	林吉特 MYR	46.371	46.164	46.642	46.137	46.255	46.319
	卢布 RUB	438.96	434.90	438.96	429.00	433.04	444.05
4月 Apr	美元 USD	655.27	649.90	655.27	649.90	652.92	656.99
	欧元 EUR	928.29	963.48	964.45	928.29	944.44	911.52
	日元 JPY	7.8532	7.9718	7.9809	7.6619	7.8460	7.9584
	港币 HKD	84.237	83.639	84.267	83.639	83.996	84.401
	英镑 GBP	1 050.27	1 081.30	1 085.18	1 050.27	1 069.44	1 058.19
	林吉特 MYR	46.196	45.655	46.369	45.538	46.118	46.270
	卢布 RUB	434.08	423.11	435.40	423.11	429.84	440.54

外币/100人民币（林吉特、卢布）
人民币元/100外币（其他7种币种）
Foreign Currency per 100 RMB (MYR、RUB)
RMB per 100 Foreign Currency (Other 7 Currency)

月份 Month	币种 Currency	期初价 Beginning of Period	期末价 End of Period	最高价 Highest	最低价 Lowest	期平均 Period Average	累计平均 Accumulative Average
5月 May	美元 USD	650.02	648.45	651.08	648.45	649.88	655.47
	欧元 EUR	961.64	932.15	964.13	913.07	931.00	915.70
	日元 JPY	8.0175	8.0214	8.0919	7.9076	8.0084	7.9691
	港币 HKD	83.677	83.368	83.738	83.353	83.590	84.227
	英镑 GBP	1 080.04	1 071.30	1 080.04	1 046.95	1 061.44	1 058.89
	林吉特 MYR	45.722	46.396	47.038	45.722	46.383	46.294
	卢布 RUB	421.42	428.09	438.14	420.71	429.90	438.26
6月 Jun	美元 USD	648.37	647.16	648.92	646.83	647.78	654.11
	欧元 EUR	934.50	936.12	950.58	913.56	931.61	918.50
	日元 JPY	7.9662	8.0243	8.1048	7.9662	8.0423	7.9820
	港币 HKD	83.370	83.162	83.398	82.942	83.201	84.046
	英镑 GBP	1 067.38	1 039.86	1 067.38	1 031.08	1 050.83	1 057.47
	林吉特 MYR	46.422	46.776	47.180	46.361	46.764	46.377
	卢布 RUB	431.35	432.88	437.26	427.78	432.17	437.19
7月 Jul	美元 USD	646.85	644.42	647.48	644.26	646.14	652.91
	欧元 EUR	936.44	922.33	941.14	906.65	923.85	919.31
	日元 JPY	8.0056	8.2846	8.2846	7.9603	8.1321	8.0046
	港币 HKD	83.105	82.696	83.170	82.694	82.960	83.883
	英镑 GBP	1 036.25	1 053.82	1 058.84	1 029.72	1 042.58	1 055.23
	林吉特 MYR	46.638	45.791	46.757	45.709	46.343	46.372
	卢布 RUB	431.75	423.56	438.38	423.56	432.14	436.43
8月 Aug	美元 USD	643.99	638.67	644.51	638.49	640.90	651.22
	欧元 EUR	925.99	921.22	926.70	907.20	918.76	919.23
	日元 JPY	8.2685	8.3296	8.3493	8.1568	8.3075	8.0473
	港币 HKD	82.642	81.923	82.681	81.923	82.194	83.645
	英镑 GBP	1 059.69	1 041.77	1 059.69	1 033.13	1 048.72	1 054.31
	林吉特 MYR	45.880	46.672	47.306	45.770	46.571	46.400
	卢布 RUB	429.41	452.72	463.70	429.41	448.73	438.17

2011年1-12月人民币市场汇率汇总表

Transaction Mid Rates of RMB in 2011

月份 Month	币种 Currency	期初价 Beginning of Period	期末价 End of Period	最高价 Highest	最低价 Lowest	期平均 Period Average	累计平均 Accumulative Average
9月 Sep	美元 USD	638.59	635.49	639.82	635.49	638.33	649.75
	欧元 EUR	917.33	863.28	917.33	856.34	880.10	914.76
	日元 JPY	8.3031	8.2978	8.3730	8.2411	8.3100	8.0773
	港币 HKD	81.995	81.539	82.069	81.539	81.889	83.444
	英镑 GBP	1 036.97	992.70	1 036.97	984.51	1 007.88	1 049.01
	林吉特 MYR	46.617	49.934	49.988	46.493	48.207	46.606
	卢布 RUB	452.42	500.85	507.69	452.42	479.52	442.89
10月 Oct	美元 USD	635.86	632.33	637.62	632.33	635.66	648.62
	欧元 EUR	853.45	894.65	897.26	853.45	878.09	911.83
	日元 JPY	8.2778	8.3520	8.3520	8.2430	8.2999	8.0951
	港币 HKD	81.708	81.441	81.983	81.441	81.739	83.308
	英镑 GBP	990.07	1 018.87	1 018.87	989.39	1 006.09	1 045.58
	林吉特 MYR	49.546	48.362	49.641	48.362	49.101	46.806
	卢布 RUB	506.17	469.02	506.17	469.02	486.68	446.39
11月 Nov	美元 USD	632.93	634.82	635.87	631.65	634.08	647.18
	欧元 EUR	876.83	846.25	876.83	845.24	860.18	906.71
	日元 JPY	8.0695	8.1314	8.2598	8.0695	8.1736	8.1029
	港币 HKD	81.478	81.500	81.639	81.312	81.482	83.127
	英镑 GBP	1 017.40	990.86	1 017.57	982.80	1 002.39	1 041.30
	林吉特 MYR	48.665	49.834	50.610	48.665	49.754	47.098
	卢布 RUB	477.79	491.93	495.35	477.79	485.99	450.31
	澳元 AUD	624.91	637.52	637.52	624.91	630.33	630.33
	加元 CAD	610.48	615.28	615.28	610.48	613.32	613.32
12月 Dec	美元 USD	633.53	630.09	634.21	630.09	632.81	645.88
	欧元 EUR	851.46	816.25	853.64	814.98	833.47	900.11
	日元 JPY	8.1609	8.1103	8.1609	8.0804	8.1261	8.1050
	港币 HKD	81.500	81.070	81.537	81.070	81.364	82.968
	英镑 GBP	994.64	971.16	994.64	971.16	986.83	1 036.39
	林吉特 MYR	49.537	50.279	50.410	49.366	49.904	47.351
	卢布 RUB	483.98	508.60	508.60	483.98	496.86	454.51
	澳元 AUD	647.63	640.93	650.49	628.15	640.38	639.17
	加元 CAD	622.14	617.77	627.68	608.83	618.22	617.63

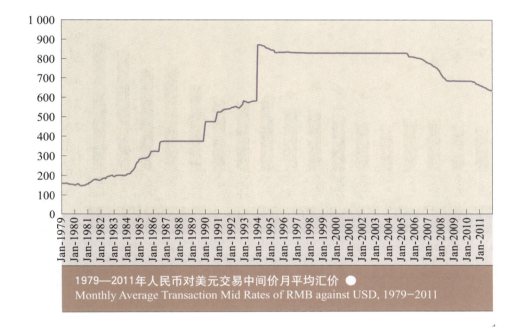

1979—2011年人民币对美元交易中间价月平均汇价 ●
Monthly Average Transaction Mid Rates of RMB against USD, 1979−2011

人民币元/100美元
RMB per 100 USD

四、利用外资①

Ⅳ. Foreign Investment Utilization

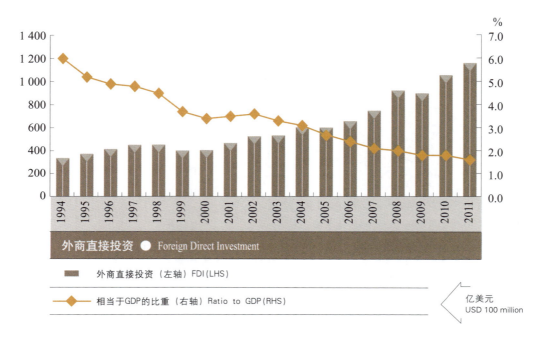

外商直接投资 ● Foreign Direct Investment

■ 外商直接投资（左轴）FDI(LHS)

◆ 相当于GDP的比重（右轴）Ratio to GDP(RHS)

亿美元
USD 100 million

①资料来源：商务部。
Sources：Ministry of Commerce.

2011年利用外资

Foreign Direct Investment in 2011

单位：亿美元
Unit: USD 100 million

利用外资方式 Mode of Foreign Investment Utilization	本年批准外资项目数 Approved Foreign Investment Programs		本年实际使用外资 Actual Utilization of Foreign Investment	
	本年累计 Accumulative in This Year	同比增长（%） Increase	本年累计 Accumulative in This Year	同比增长（%） Increase
总计 Total	27 712	1.12	1 176.98	8.16
一、外商直接投资 Direct Foreign Investment	27 712	1.12	1 160.11	9.72
中外合资企业 Sino-Foreign Equity Joint Venture	5 005	0.7	214.15	−4.81
中外合作企业 Sino-Foreign Contractual Joint Venture	284	−5.33	17.57	8.69
外资企业 Foreign Investment Enterprise	22 388	1.37	912.05	12.63
外商投资股份制 Stock-Holding by Foreign Investment	35	−31.37	16.34	152.83
合作开发 Cooperation Exploitation	0		0	
其他 Others	0		0	
二、外商其他投资 Other Foreign Investment	0		16.87	−45.32
对外发行股票 Issue Stocks to the Outside	0		9.39	43.56
国际租赁 International Tenancy	0		0	−100
补偿贸易 Compensation Trade	0		0.54	20.77
加工装配 Processing & Assembling	0		6.94	−35.59

注：统计数据为非金融领域。
Note：The data is subject to non-financial sectors.

五、外债①
V. External Debt

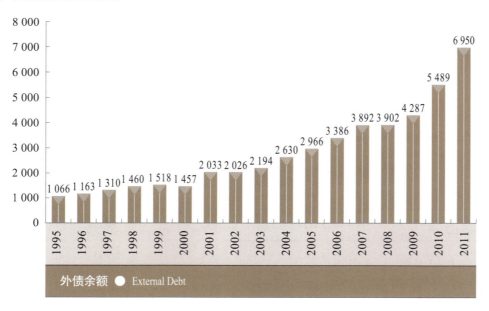

外债余额 ● External Debt

亿美元
USD 100 million

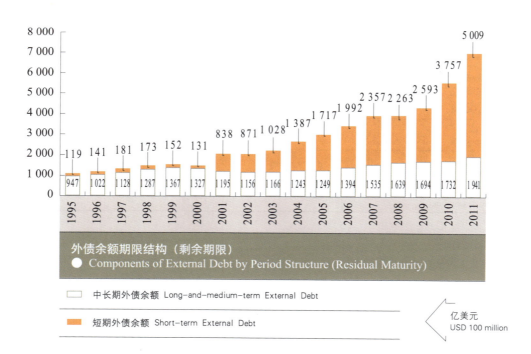

外债余额期限结构（剩余期限）
● Components of External Debt by Period Structure (Residual Maturity)

□ 中长期外债余额 Long-and-medium-term External Debt

 短期外债余额 Short-term External Debt

亿美元
USD 100 million

①资料来源：国家外汇管理局。
Sources：State Administration of Foreign Exchange.

2011年末外债余额期限结构（剩余期限）
Components of External Debt by Period Structure（Residual Maturity），End—2011

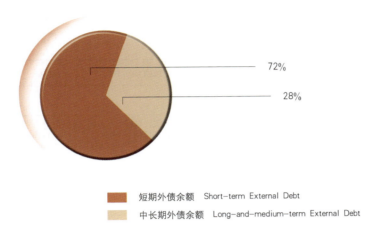

72%

28%

■ 短期外债余额　Short-term External Debt
■ 中长期外债余额　Long-and-medium-term External Debt

2011年末登记外债余额主体结构
Components of Registered External Debt by Type of Debtor，End—2011

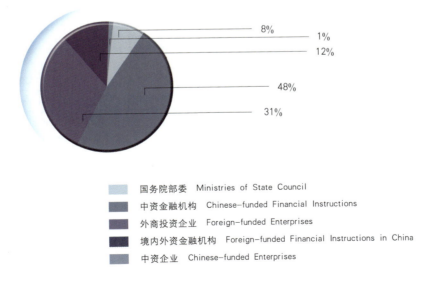

8%　1%

12%

48%

31%

■ 国务院部委　Ministries of State Council
■ 中资金融机构　Chinese-funded Financial Instructions
■ 外商投资企业　Foreign-funded Enterprises
■ 境内外资金融机构　Foreign-funded Financial Instructions in China
■ 中资企业　Chinese-funded Enterprises

六、国际旅游

VI. International Tourism

入境过夜旅游者人数和旅游外汇收入

Number of Inbound Stay-over Tourists and Foreign Exchange Income from Tourism

年份 Year	入境过夜旅游(万人次) Inbound Stay-over Tourists(10 000 persons)	旅游外汇收入（亿美元） Foreign Exchange Income from Tourism(USD 100 million)	年份 Year	入境过夜旅游（万人次） Inbound Stay-over Tourists(10 000 persons)	旅游外汇收入（亿美元） Foreign Exchange Income from Tourism(USD 100 million)
1978	71.6	2.63	1995	2 003.4	87.33
1979	152.9	4.49	1996	2 276.5	102.00
1980	350.0	6.17	1997	2 377.0	120.74
1981	367.7	7.85	1998	2 507.3	126.02
1982	392.4	8.43	1999	2 704.7	140.99
1983	379.1	9.41	2000	3 122.9	162.24
1984	514.1	11.31	2001	3 316.7	177.92
1985	713.3	12.50	2002	3 680.3	203.85
1986	900.1	15.31	2003	3 297.1	174.06
1987	1 076.0	18.62	2004	4 176.1	257.39
1988	1 236.1	22.47	2005	4 680.9	292.96
1989	936.1	18.60	2006	4 991.0	339.49
1990	1 048.4	22.18	2007	5 472.0	419.19
1991	1 246.4	28.45	2008	5 304.9	408.43
1992	1 651.2	39.47	2009	5 087.5	396.75
1993	1 898.2	46.83	2010	5 566.5	519.75
1994	2 107.0	73.23	2011	5 758.1	596.82

①资料来源：国家旅游局。
Sources：China National Tourism Administration.

七、世界经济增长状况①
Ⅶ. Growth of World Economy

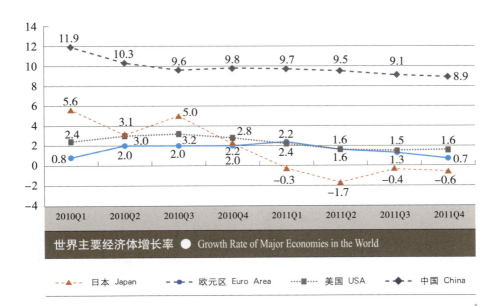

世界主要经济体增长率 ● Growth Rate of Major Economies in the World

--▲-- 日本 Japan　　--●-- 欧元区 Euro Area　　······■······ 美国 USA　　--◆-- 中国 China

经济增长率(%)
Growth Rate of Economy (%)

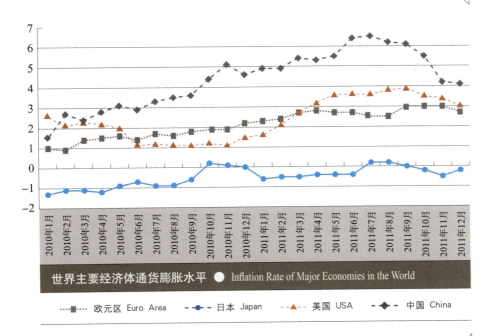

世界主要经济体通货膨胀水平 ○ Inflation Rate of Major Economies in the World

······■······ 欧元区 Euro Area　　--●-- 日本 Japan　　--▲-- 美国 USA　　--◆-- 中国 China

①资料来源：彭博资讯，CEIC Asia Database。
Sources: Bloomberg, CEIC Asia Database.

居民消费价格指数
CPI（%）

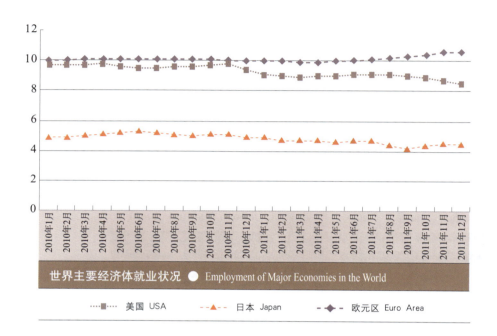

世界主要经济体就业状况 ● Employment of Major Economies in the World

········■········ 美国 USA   – –▲– – 日本 Japan   – –◆– – 欧元区 Euro Area

失业率(%)
Unemployment Rate (%)

八、国际金融市场状况^①

Ⅷ．International Financial Market

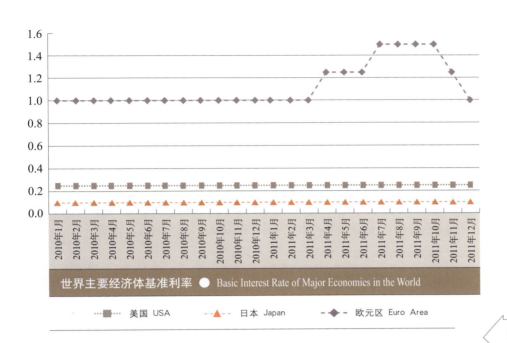

世界主要经济体基准利率 ● Basic Interest Rate of Major Economies in the World

····■···· 美国 USA 　—▲— 日本 Japan 　–◆– 欧元区 Euro Area

基准利率(%)
Basic Interest Rate (%)

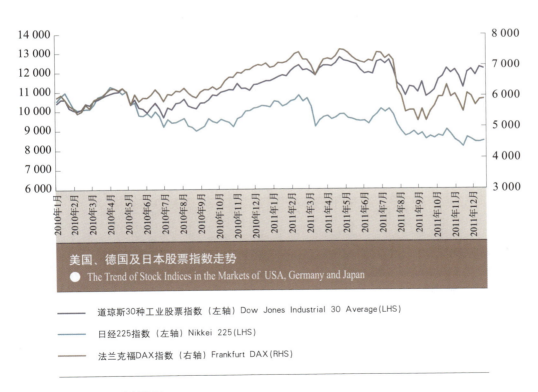

美国、德国及日本股票指数走势
○ The Trend of Stock Indices in the Markets of USA, Germany and Japan

——— 道琼斯30种工业股票指数（左轴）Dow Jones Industrial 30 Average(LHS)

——— 日经225指数（左轴）Nikkei 225(LHS)

——— 法兰克福DAX指数（右轴）Frankfurt DAX(RHS)

①资料来源：彭博资讯。
Sources：Bloomberg.

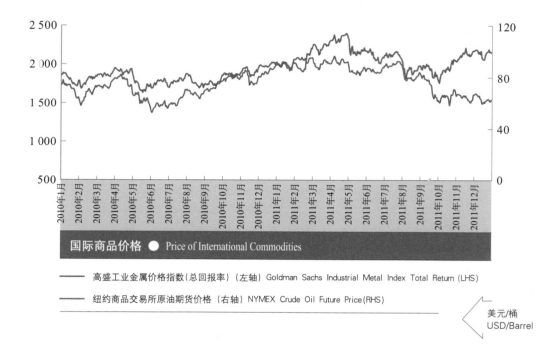

国际商品价格 ● Price of International Commodities

—— 高盛工业金属价格指数（总回报率）（左轴）Goldman Sachs Industrial Metal Index Total Return (LHS)

—— 纽约商品交易所原油期货价格（右轴）NYMEX Crude Oil Future Price (RHS)

美元/桶
USD/Barrel

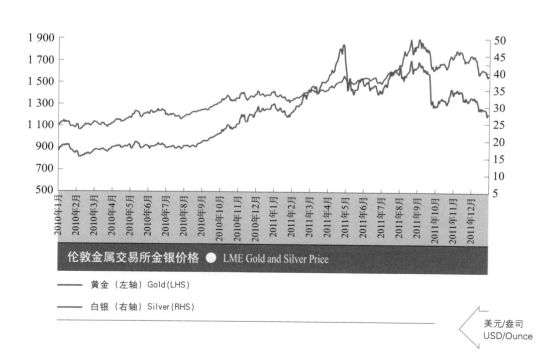

伦敦金属交易所金银价格 ● LME Gold and Silver Price

—— 黄金（左轴）Gold(LHS)

—— 白银（右轴）Silver (RHS)

美元/盎司
USD/Ounce